CLEARCUTTING

A VIEW
FROM
THE TOP

CLEARCUTTING:

A VIEW FROM THE TOP

WITH CHAPTERS BY

Lee M. James, Michigan State Univ. Department of Forestry; **Robert E. Dils,** Colorado State Univ. College of Forestry; **Charles W. Ralston,** Duke Univ. School of Forestry; **James S. Bethel,** Univ. of Washington College of Forest Resources; **W. W. Ward,** Pennsylvania State Univ. School of Forest Resources; **Ernest M. Gould, Jr.,** of Harvard Univ.

ELEANOR C. J. HORWITZ

ACROPOLIS BOOKS ON CURRENT ISSUES

PUBLISHED BY **ACROPOLIS BOOKS LTD.** • WASHINGTON, D.C. 20009

ACROPOLIS BOOKS LTD.

Colortone Building, 2400 17th St., N.W.
Washington, D.C. 20009

Printed in the United States of America by
COLORTONE PRESS Creative Graphics Inc., *Washington, D. C. 20009*

Library of Congress Cataloging in Publication Data

Horwitz, Eleanor C   J   1939–
    Clearcutting: a view from the top.

    Bibliography: p.
    1. Clear-cutting—United States. I. Title.
SD538.2.A1H67   333.7'5   73-7948
ISBN 0-87491-364-0
ISBN 0-87491-363-2 (pbk.)

ᴄᵢᴘ

Preface

This book began as a seedling when, as a conservation specialist for an Oregon school system, I became aware of how little the majority of people in that locality knew about the major industry of their particular area. Concern was growing but, all too often, facts were few. Since that time I have noted sadly that people in other parts of the nation often consider clearcutting a local issue which is of little interest to them. They are oblivious to the fact that this controversy and its outcomes affect one of their nation's most important resources, not to mention their pocketbooks and their future.

The fault is not theirs alone. The information they should have has not been made available to them. Most of the material on clearcutting is either highly technical or excessively charged with emotion. Sound facts presented in a straightforward way, with the evaluation left to the reader, are hard to come by. There was a need for material to fill this gap, and so the idea of the book matured.

Many people have contributed in a variety of ways to the process of helping this book to grow. A few deserve special mention. My thanks are due to the authors, the five deans and Dr. Gould, who permitted the use of their material and provided comments and assistance throughout the condensation process. I would like to extend thanks also to Dr. Robert Pierce of the U.S. Forest Service, project leader of the experiment at Hubbard Brook, for his cooperation and assistance on the chapter "Hubbard Brook Revisited."

A large vote of thanks is due James Patric of the U.S. Timber and Watershed Laboratory and to Dr. Douglas Gilbert, Assistant Dean of Forestry, Colorado State University, for their encouragement and editorial aid; to Dave Burwell for pictures; to Gene Bergoffen, U.S. Forest Service specialist in legislative affairs; and to Dick Wilson for good humor when the going got rough. Finally a special note of thanks to Jacqueline Rudd for typing, baby-sitting and tea, all when they were most needed.

—E.H.

Contents

Introduction

THE CONTROVERSY OVER WHETHER or not to permit clearcutting is certainly not a new one on the American scene. During the 1920s and 1930s, when this nation first began to think about conservation in an organized way and when the Forest Service was still very young, professional foresters were already debating the relative merits and liabilities of this particular form of logging. At first the controversy was limited primarily to argument among forestry professionals; people who were not professionally concerned with timber management seemed to have been largely indifferent to the issue. And so it continued for almost half a century. Then in the late 1960's, all that changed.

Suddenly there was a surge of general interest in anything which related to our natural environment. Spurred on perhaps by the photographs of our planet taken by orbitting astronauts, people suddenly became more aware of the importance and the fragility of this tiny Earth. Warnings which had been sounded years before by such conservationists as Barry Commoner and William Vogt now carried new impact. Recreationists headed for the forests in increasing numbers and many concerned citizens developed a feeling of personal responsibility for our vital natural resources.

As the environmental movement gained popularity and more was said and written about various aspects of the management and mismanagement of natural resources, legislators began to turn their attention toward conservation issues which had not seemed so pressing before.

Photographs such as this one, taken by the crew of Apollo 11 in 1969, may have contributed materially to the growth of popular appreciation of the planet Earth: small, finite, and precious for its ability to support life. Photo, NASA

Responding to the active concern of the American people, President Richard Nixon established an Environmental Protection Agency and a Council on Environmental Quality. These were but two of the many public agencies whose task in the late 1960's was to keep tabs on environmental matters and to make recommendations for action whenever that was indicated.

As people spent more time in the nation's forests, they inevitably came in contact with forest harvest. To many of them the act and the ugliness of the results became a matter of profound concern and even outrage. Thus in 1971, in response to considerable public outcry, serious consideration was given to an executive order which would have banned all clearcutting, at least temporarily, from publicly owned lands. Emotions ran high, but few hard facts were available to the legislative groups concerned with the problem.

As a partial response to the lack of information, a committee of the National Academy of Sciences (NAS), headed by Dr. David Gates of the University of Michigan, began investigating the clearcutting practices in the Bitterroot National Forest of Montana—an area in which clearcutting had been loudly denounced by some prominent botanists. The report of this committee, as yet unpublished, should become available by 1974.

At the same time four federal agencies began gathering data and conducting hearings regarding forestry practices on public lands in general; clearcutting in particular.

Under the leadership of Senator Frank Church (D-Idaho), a subcommittee of the Senate Committee on Interior and Insular Affairs began a series of hearings on the topic of management practices on the public lands. From April to September 1971, the Church subcommittee heard testimony relating primarily to clearcutting from foresters, biologists, and interested private citizens. In the end the committee issued a full report on its hearings—but found that there was not enough evidence to support the proposal to ban clearcutting. Instead, the committee issued a set of guidelines for logging which have since been

11

adopted by the United States Forest Service and which are publicly available in that organization's action plan.

Not long after this, another investigative organization was established: a panel on Timber and the Environment chaired by ex-Secretary of the Interior Fred Seaton. This committee, consisting of Secretary Seaton, Dr. Donald Zinn (University of Rhode Island), Dr. Steven Spurr (University of Texas), Dr. Marion Clawson (Resources for the Future) and Mr. Ralph Hodges (National Forest Products Institute), was charged with the task of compiling hard information on the nature of forestry and forest cutting, and reporting directly to the President with recommendations, if any, on action to be initiated. Their report was released during September of 1973.

In 1972, a special committee composed of the Secretaries of Interior and Agriculture as well as the Chairman of the Council on Environmental Quality recommended against the proposed moratorium on clearcutting, and no further official action was taken pending the reports of the other committees.

During this time the Council on Environmental Quality, in its quest for unbiased, factual information, commissioned the deans of forestry schools at five major universities to compile reports on the status of clearcutting in their individual areas. The deans chosen to participate in this project were selected to represent the different forested areas around the nation. Each was requested to focus his report on clearcutting as it affected the forest types peculiar to his region—specifically in the public forests.

Dr. W. W. Ward, Director of the School of Forest Resources of the Pennsylvania State University was charged with the task of distilling the material relevant to forests of the Northeastern United States. Dr. Charles W. Ralston, Dean of the School of Forestry at Duke University, did the same for the Southeastern forests, with particular emphasis on the pine forests. Dr. Lee M. James, Chairman of the Department of Forestry at Michigan State University, was selected to examine clearcutting in the

12

forests of the North Central region, while Dr. Robert E. Dils, a leading forest hydrologist and presently Dean of the College of Forestry and Natural Resources at Colorado State University, undertook to examine the status of cutting in the public forests of the Rocky Mountain region. The forests of the Far West, primarily those of Oregon, Washington and Alaska, fell to Dr. James S. Bethel, Dean of the College of Forest Resources of the University of Washington. Using the resources available through their respective universities, the authors were able to tap much of the most important thinking of foresters both in the field and in the universities of their region. Their detailed reports are presently on record with the Council on Environmental Quality.

These reports are of especial value in that they focus in great detail on the problems of clearcutting in a given region while maintaining and presenting a broad view of the problem of clearcutting on a national scale. Because of this, they have been distilled into shortened form with their author's consent[1] to give the reader an overview of some of the current professional thinking on this controversial matter.

The Deans' reports are presented here together with additional material which will help the reader to view the issue in perspective as he forms his own evaluation. An initial explanation of clearcutting and an indication of some of the problems involved serve as an introduction to those not already fully familiar with this harvest technique. This is followed by the five reports.

During the past years one "clearcut" has been held up time and again as an example to damn the whole practice. It is an experimental cut performed in the Hubbard Brook Experimental Forest of New Hampshire in 1966. This experiment in watershed values, not in clearcutting as such, has been quoted and misquoted many times; it has appeared every major discussion of clearcutting since that time.

---

[1]One report, that from the Southeast, is presented in its entirety as it was considerably shorter than the others.

To understand the experiment it is important to know the aim of the experiment, the conditions under which the operation was performed and the status of the forest some eight years later. In "Hubbard Brook Revisited" we have presented the basic facts relating to this experiment so that the reader may have a background against which to view the references to the "cut" which appear throughout the literature on clearcutting.

Finally, because forest harvest is both a biological and an economic issue, and because the two are inextricably intertwined, a chapter has been included on the economics of clearcutting by Dr. Ernest M. Gould, Jr., Forest Economist, Harvard University. This chapter puts the entire controversy in place in the broad context of social and economic values which must be considered.

The Deans' reports are a matter of public record; other reports will be available soon. The controversy over clearcutting is far from dead. In parts of the country where forest products form an important part of the economic base, tempers still flare over harvesting methods. In these areas the debate over clearcutting still ranks as the number one conservation controversy. As this book goes to press, the NAS committee is preparing its statement and recommendations, while the Seaton report is studied by presidential advisors. Once these reports are digested, the matter may once again be opened to review. This time, however, much more factual information will be available, although still more might be desired.

It is hoped that this book, along with the official reports, will aid in stripping away the emotionalism which has characterized the clearcutting debate and that it will serve as a springboard for any who wish to go on to inform themselves in greater depth about this most important resource controversy.

1 The Problem- A Matter of Definitions, Methods and Priorities

What *is* a clearcut? Surely a book on clearcutting should open with a neat, concise definition of the trouble spot involved. The task, however, is a very difficult one. To date there is no fully accepted and established definition of a clearcut, even after three years of heated controversy. This lack of agreement on a definition is in itself part of the problem. Every participant in the debate has his own personal definition of what clearcutting is and what a clearcut looks like. Usually a speaker or writer assumes that everyone in his audience shares his particular definition with all its attendant connotations. Here is where the trouble begins. Often as not violent opponents can agree on whether a particular operation is a good one or a disaster. But is this example typical or accidental? Is the clearcut method primarily useful or harmful? The differing answers to these questions lie at the root of the lack of communication which has characterized the clearcutting debate.

Basically a clearcut might be defined as a tree cutting operation in which all the trees on a given area of land are felled in a short period of time. At this point agreement ends and the widely disparate connotations enter to color the picture of the clearcut. The definition is, at best, vague and open to many interpretations.

"...All the trees...are felled...." Just what does this

15

really mean? In any logging operation some trees, those below a particular height or diameter, remain. Where the remaining trees are tall and stout, the cut is classified as a non-clearcut. A clearcut is one in which no trees remain which are apparent. Some trees *do* remain, however, on any cutover area. No area is fully cleared. Grasses, flowers and shrubs are left and in among them are the very youngest trees. In a few years these trees will stand taller than the surrounding vegetation—does their presence make the foregoing cut not a clearcut? How large must the leftover trees be before the area is considered not to have been clearcut?

How large or small is the "given area of land" involved? Even the most extreme opponent of cutting would not argue that the felling of three large trees constitutes a clearcut. Where, then, does clearcutting begin? Is the envisioned cut one acre? Five acres? Five hundred acres? A cutover area of a single acre might be classified as a patch cutting; beyond that the division between patch and clearcut is unclear. One acre is acceptable. One square mile is an atrocity. Obviously attitudes toward clearcutting depend greatly on the size of the cutover area in question. It is important to define that "given area of land."

What constitutes "a short period of time"? If an area is logged completely in a matter of days, that is considered a clearcut. Is it still a clearcut if half the trees are removed within a few days and the other half is removed a year or more later, after regrowth has become established? There is a spectrum of methods of cutting ranging from direct clearing, through seedtree methods, "shelterwood," and finally grading into a "thinning" cut. Some of these are clearcut methods, others are not. Even professional foresters are often hard put to define cuts which fall between the extremes. Somehow, time of cutting is a factor in determining what is a clearcut. But how far apart in time must two cuts be to be considered unrelated, rather than two halves of the same operation?

Clearly the degree of tree removal, size of the area, time scale of removal and the nature of the area all combine in the

16

Where clearcuts are too large, the scenery is barren and monotonous.

definition of a clearcut. The precise nature of each factor influences whether the cutting is seen as beneficial or evil, and determines whether clearcutting carries the connotation of super-harvest, rape or something in between.

In fact, forest clearing is, as it has always been, a tool; it is neither demon nor panacea. How it affects the land depends entirely on the nature of that land and the way in which the clearing has been carried out. Like any tool, it has been and can be used to serve many purposes.

In the earliest days of a nation's development, clearcutting is used primarily as a form of forest removal; and so it was in this country. Clearing eliminated the forest so that land was available for farms, roads and growing towns. At this stage there was no concern for the forest—it was an obstacle to be overcome quickly and efficiently.

Later, clearcutting was conducted for wood rather than for land, but the harvest was carried out for immediate economic gain with no special concern for the land or for the forest of the future. Clearcutting was an inexpensive way of getting a great deal of wood from a small area. If the forest was damaged, what of it? There were more and better forests further west. Little thought was expended on such things as forest regeneration. Forest restoration brought no financial gain.

Lack of concern for the health of the forest went along with the early clearing operations, but it was by no means limited to them. During the 19th century the same lack of concern was general to logging operations. At that time a practice became common in which loggers entered an area, cut only those trees which would bring high economic returns, and left. The desirable species which they had removed were subsequently crowded out by less desirable species which the loggers had rejected. This pernicious practice, known as "highgrading," or more colloquially "cut out and get out," stripped many United States forests of black walnut, cherry and other prime trees. Such logging persists to this day hidden under the cloak of selection management. There are still loggers who take only what is commercially useful, leaving inferior, unhealthy trees to take over the area. Such cutting is both harmful and uneconomical and deserves a full measure of public indignation.

During the 19th century, private commercial enterprises worked the forests over to provide wood for farmsteads in the Northeast, wood for the coking of steel mills in the South, and wood for building the corrals, fences and railroads of the expanding West. The forests which remained after the first quality trees had been cut were generally scrubby. Because they were considered worthless, many of these forest lands were sold cheaply after 1914. They were bought by the federal government, and the rejected land became the base for the present National Forest system.

Sixty years of protection and selective cutting have promoted regeneration of desirable species, many of which are now close to the point of maturity. The methods which have brought them to this point were designed specifically to bring back land abused by unsound practices. That land has been restored. Management must now be aimed at dealing with restored lands to preserve the values which are deemed most important. By now, high-grading and similar forms of exploitation are coming to an end in the United States. Forest technology has become highly sophisticated. Simple logging has given way to forest management; its goal is to preserve forest soil productivity and to stimulate rapid regrowth of the forest after it has been cut. The professional know-how which will make logging into "good logging" exists. Now it is essential that loggers be made to practice what foresters preach, and to log in harmony with the many uses of a piece of land. This is most easily and best done on private timber lands. These lands have one purpose— maximum timber production—and their continued productivity is economically vital to their logger-owner. Thus private logging holdings are often among the best managed and least controversial areas. The areas needing greatest protection are the public lands. These are used for many purposes, including recreation, wildlife management, and water protection as well as

timber, hence the disagreement over their major "use." The danger to these lands lies in the fact that they are cut by loggers who have no particular stake in the growth return, for they will not have a chance to gain from that area again. To date it has been to the logger's advantage to cut on public lands with the minimum of expense—and restoration can be expensive. Protective legislation can help, but ultimately public lands will be in danger until it is made cost effective to the logger to log public lands as carefully as he would his own. How trees are best managed is still the subject of debate even among professional foresters.

Basically there are two systems for tree management—which one is preferable depends on the overall goal for the specific area. Trees can be grown in stands in which all the trees are of one species and approximately one age. Management for such stands is called "even-aged management." Under an even-age system, large areas are cleared and then either replanted or permitted to regenerate naturally. Culture is relatively simple, as trees in the stand are ready for thinning or other treatment at the same time and under the same conditions. Within the even-aged stand some trees grow more rapidly than others. The sprinkling of small trees may lead some to believe that there is a group of trees in another age class or even that these stunted trees represent new reproduction. It can easily be shown, however, that the small trees are of roughly the same age as the large ones. They together with the large trees are harvested at the point of maturity in their growth. Beyond this point trees become increasingly subject to rot and other diseases.

Trees may also be grown in a forest in which a variety of different ages and species of trees are represented—an uneven-aged stand. Such a forest has great visual and biological variety, but it is difficult and expensive to maintain. Treatments such as thinning, which might benefit young trees, are difficult to perform, as the trees to be removed might be those just approaching maturity. Logging must be selective and continuous as mature trees must periodically be removed to make way

A bullbuck, or logging foreman, places the undercut carefully so that this large Douglas fir will fall in the designated spot.   Photo, D. Burwell

for younger trees. Most important, certain tree species will not grow under this system, for the seedlings would have to grow in heavy shade provided by the existing forest.

Both systems approximate natural conditions. Even-aged management simulates the situation in areas which were cleared by natural disaster, fire, storm or disease. It does so in a controlled and orderly way. Uneven-aged management simulates a situation which is rarer; that of the forest growing undisturbed by natural forces. In nature, this latter is a stage which would usually end with a forest fire or other natural clearing event.

Where recreation is a major form of forest use, uneven-aged management may be preferred, for the uneven-aged forest is far more diverse and interesting, but the periodic logging activity needed may make such management objectionable. Even-aged management causes a few years of ugliness after harvest, and it may damage the area for some forms of recreation as well as for watershed protection. Its advantage is that the area so cut can then be left to other uses for an extended period of time. Many foresters believe that, over-all, even-aged management may be less disruptive than frequent manipulation. Clearcutting is the appropriate harvest method for timbers managed in even-aged blocks. Thus clearcutting is no longer just a method of clearing away the forest or of stripping out a quick profit; it is another silvicultural tool, to be used when and where it can be beneficial.

One of the first major attempts to use clearcutting as a tool in a well considered program of forest development in the U.S. was carried out by Gifford Pinchot. Always ahead of his time, Pinchot ordered a large-scale clearcut of yellow poplar with the intention of restoring the same forest as rapidly as possible. The cut was sound, and within a few years the area was overgrown by a new, vigorous stand of the desirable yellow poplar.

Yellow poplar is an intolerant species. It requires full sunlight for proper growth. Seedlings of intolerant species grow poorly, if at all, in the shade provided by their elders. The list of

22

A mature hardwood stand, managed under a selective logging system, is characterized by a wide variety of tree species as may be seen in this area photographed in 1973 and uncut since 1962.

intolerant species includes some of the most attractive trees in the forest. Black walnut, aspen, black cherry and white birch are but a few of the trees which need sunlight for seedling growth. These are temporary successional species which, in the ordinary course of events, would give way to shade tolerant species such as beech and hemlock unless a clearing were opened up by a fire or windstorm.

Southern pines and western Douglas fir are also intolerant. Beneath the canopy of the mature Douglas fir forest there are few small trees, none of them young Douglas fir. Douglas fir forests exist today as a result of the many forest fires which raged across the slopes of the western mountains from time to time. Today we cannot afford to permit such natural catastrophes. Modern fire detection and prevention methods make it possible to protect lives and property by halting fires as soon as they are noticed. The result is that the age-old natural balance is being tipped away from intolerant species. Because of this, management efforts must be geared toward a system in which such temporary ecological stages as the Douglas fir forest can be maintained.

Trees of the intermediate forest stages are generally managed in even-aged blocks for two reasons. The first is their intolerance. Large sunny forest openings are essential to their healthy reproduction. The second factor is their lack of resistance to environmental stresses, for despite their occasionally massive appearance, these trees have relatively soft wood and weak root systems. Unlike hard maples and oaks, the soft-wooded trees are subject to severe damage from wind, ice and a variety of rotting agents. Where some but not all in a given stand of such trees are removed, others deprived of their windbreak effect may be blown down, splintering themselves and other trees as they fall. The result of such a blowdown is severe fire hazard and often considerable economic loss.

Some shade tolerant trees share this characteristic of weak-rootedness, among them spruce and some fir types. These trees *can* grow and reproduce in shade. Because they are weak and subject to wind damage, however, they too are often managed in even-aged blocks. As a rule-of-thumb, both intolerant and/or weakly rooted trees are managed under the even-aged system. Others may be managed in uneven-aged stands.

Occasionally, attempts have been made to see whether intolerant trees can be managed by methods other than the traditional ones. On a small scale, the experiments have been successful. Jack pine and Douglas fir have been grown in shade. Large scale attempts to manage these species by selection, such as were carried out during the 1930's, proved disastrous failures.

Clearcutting is also employed as a health improvement technique for sections of forest found to be in poor condition. Forests which have been "highgraded" can be clearcut so that the removed desirable species can grow once again. This is especially applicable in the case of eastern hardwoods.

Forest sections infested with insect pests may be stripped and the wood burned as a sanitation measure. Such drastic cutting protects unaffected trees in adjacent areas. In sections of the Far West, where trees may be heavily infected with the parasitic dwarf mistletoe plant, clearcutting is the preferred way to eliminate the pest. In general, wherever a progressive form of rot or illness threatens healthy trees, complete forest removal is recommended.

Finally, clearcuts are occasionally suggested for areas in which soil disturbance and general site deterioration may be a problem; where it is important to keep road building to a minimum. Of course *any* form of logging may damage a logging site but this need not be so. Increasingly, foresters are finding that site deterioration is due to careless logging and particularly to poor road construction, rather than to the removal of nutrients taken from the land. Ordinarily old rootwads support the soil of a cutover area until regrowth is established. Where roads have been built carelessly, however, soil washes away and erosion gullies form. Water is the great carrier of all water-soluble nutrients—those needed by plants—so these trails

25

of running water form exit paths for materials which are needed on site for the next forest generation. Sediment washed through these channels may clog streams. This is especially true where roads have been laid out near stream-courses, which is often done because it is easier to build there.

Actually, two thirds of the nutrients contained in trees are left on the logging site in form of twigs, roots, leaves, "slash" and other unmarketable material. This material looks bad on the logging site. In fact, however, it provides an important nutrient material bank for the coming crop. If logging is carried out with proper care, nutrient drain should pose no problem. It will be no problem until the day arrives when the 100 percent "clean-up" or 100 percent utilization, now an experimental goal, becomes a reality.

The problem for the moment is to protect streams and to minimize soil disturbance—then nutrients will automatically be preserved on the site. Two techniques are especially helpful in attaining this goal. The first, tree pulling, is a relatively new practice currently in use on some private timber lands. With this system trees are no longer permitted to crash onto the hillside, damaging themselves and possibly others in the vicinity. Instead, a heavy steel cable is attached to the trunk of the tree. As the tree is cut, the cable is tightened until finally the tree is actually pulled over, its fall controlled by the cable. The "pulled" tree falls uphill and thus falls a shorter distance than one which falls downhill. The impact is considerably less. Tree pulling is expensive but some loggers are convinced that it is justified both in terms of wood saved (pulled trees are not shattered by the impact of the fall nor do they have badly broken tops) and in terms of the lessened damage to the ground below.

After the trees are felled and bucked, they must be yarded. At one time this was done by skidding logs down the hillsides to a road halfway down the slope or even at the edge of a stream. Today, in most operations, logs are yarded uphill by tough steel cables to roads located along the ridge tops.

27

This large "witch's broom" is caused by dwarf mistletoe, an infectious parasitic growth. The presence of dwarf mistletoe in such species as lodgepole pine or Douglas fir is often a factor in the decision to use clearcutting as a method of harvest. Photo C. R. Batten

The advantages of this system are many. Pulled logs damage the soil less than do wildly sliding ones. They are controlled by a cable and so pose no danger to the men working on the slopes. Most important, pulling logs uphill means that roads can be kept far from streambeds and other sensitive areas, making it truly practical to leave and maintain protective buffer strips.

As long as roads are a hazard to the condition of the logged area, it makes sense to harvest using the minimum amount of road for the shortest possible period of time. This suggests even-aged management, for the more concentrated the logging operation, the fewer miles of road are needed for the transport of logs to market. Where a cut is completed quickly and further logging is not needed, the road can be permitted to "decay"—in some operations reversion is encouraged by planting grass on the road after the job is completed.

Where clearcutting is practiced for biologically sound reasons, it can enhance other forest values. Among these is the supply of feed for animals. For pleasant as they may be to human wanderers, old growth coniferous forests are often poor feeding areas for many forms of wildlife. Little light penetrates the dense. canopy and forage at ground level is scarce. Clearings, if appropriately placed and timed, can do much to provide feed for deer, moose, grouse, rabbit and other animals. To do this cuts must be spaced correctly over winter and summer ranges, wherever extra food is needed. The clearings should not destroy areas inhabited primarily by "old-forest" animals such as squirrels, raccoons or wild turkeys. They must not be so large that animals cannot easily run from the food-rich centers to the safety of the surrounding forest, but they must not be so small that they focus an inordinate amount of foraging on a limited area.

CLEARCUTTING AS A SOCIAL PROBLEM

To be sure, we still need to learn many things about the specific effects of clearcutting. In time research may provide some

Although logging slash is unsightly, it is vital as a nutrient bank as well as for ground protection. Photo, D. Burwell

29

answers to the questions and uncertainties which now trouble foresters. Perhaps someday the disciplines of forest science and botany will have specific, prescriptive answers to the questions "Where should we clearcut?" or "What is the best treatment for this area?" But scientific research can shed light only on the objective aspects of the problem. The major issue remains that of public attitudes and esthetic feelings.

There is no way to deny a fresh clearcut is *ugly*! Whether regrowth will maintain soil and cover logging scars in one year, 10 or 20 years is not the important question. What matters is that, like a new haircut, the clearcut is embarassingly evident. For this reason it has become a symbol of man's injury, real and fancied, to the natural world. As a symbol, clearcutting has been attacked and defended with a vehemence far beyond that of simple scientific controversy.

To many opponents, clearcutting is tantamount to a systematic conversion of forest to desert. In support of this theory there are historical examples from the once-forested Middle East, from portions of Africa and from the Balkans. Indeed, today these dry, scrubby lands stand as evidence of man's misplaced goals. To view these examples in perspective however, one must look beyond mere forest cutting and note the aim of the loggers and the uses to which the land was put after logging. In each case these lands were cleared with forest removal at least a partial goal. Once opened, the land was used for grazing of livestock—primarily sheep and goats. Could the areas have grown back? It is not likely that these early loggers had any intention of allowing even the most marginal agricultural land to revert to forest. Thus these areas were not merely cut but, like the watershed at Hubbard Brook, they were effectively defoliated—not for three years but for several hundred. Was it the cutting method or the grazing which caused the barrenness evident today? The present-day forests of Scandinavia, Germany and Japan, long managed under the even-aged system, may provide a partial answer. Climate and post-cutting treatment, rather than cutting method, must have a decisive effect.

What are the possible effects of clearcutting on the forests of the United States? Opinions and emotions run high but facts are often scarce. Arguments may be based on shreds of evidence seen and interpreted by non-professionals. Rarely are these people acquainted in more than a passing manner with the rather formidable body of knowledge which is modern forest science. They should not be expected to be experts, for forestry has become a highly complex and technical professional field. But where public interest has become focused on a forestry issue, it is imperative that professional foresters, whether public, industrial or academic, get out and explain the reasoning behind their practices to the interested public. Too often the foresters' concerns as well as their findings are discussed only with each other at professional meetings. It is up to the professionals to strip away the misinformation which persists about forestry practice and to provide facts to replace the emotionalism which has characterized much of the controversy to date.

The question of clearcutting—when, where and whether—is far more complex, however, than it appears at first glance. It is not merely a matter of getting the facts to people who may be ignorant of them. It is not a conflict between Good and Evil, as it is occasionally presented. It is ultimately, as are many natural resource conflicts, a disagreement about relative priorities and values. Ironically, many antagonists in this controversy share the same values, but their priorities are arranged differently. With them, we are all trapped in a mesh of conflicting wants.

We want to provide recreational opportunities for even more people who enjoy leisure time given them by an advancing standard of living. We encourage people from all walks of life to care for and about our natural resources; thus we should not be surprised at the rising recreational pressure placed on forest lands.

We want to maintain wilderness, pristine and distant. We

31

32   *Good second growth Douglas fir forests are often considered desirable sites for "second homes." The stumps near the cabin stand as evidence of previous logging in the forest.*

want this for the hardy few who enjoy these areas despite the difficult access, as well as for those who may never see wilderness but who feel a sense of awe just knowing that it still exists. We want wilderness for "just in case"—areas to remain untouched unless and until they become essential.

We want adequate housing for all—and the standard of adequacy is constantly rising. It has been suggested that we provide for this "want" with some material other than wood. But what material would it be? Metals must be mined and refined; plastics must be synthesized chemically. Either would require a major additional expenditure of energy, in an energy budget which is already heavily burdened. Each would create another set of serious environmental problems. If we consider shifting the basic building material (no one has yet suggested giving up the goal of adequate housing), which of our values would be jeopardized by the switch?

We want employment opportunities for all and job security where possible. Admittedly the number of workers employed by an industry is no indication of that industry's desirability. A shift away from wood, however, would cause serious economic dislocation in some areas and would require both careful planning and gradual implementation.

We want tax revenues to be available to areas which have natural resources but which lack heavy, tax-producing industries. Such areas are among the most attractive and pleasant in the nation. At this time they often depend heavily on timber revenue taxes.

We want inexpensive materials with which to "play." We are a nation of do-it-yourselfers and basement carpenters. Wood is essential for many of these basic hobby and home improvement needs.

We expect communication on paper at a price all can afford. The exchange of facts and ideas has long been basic to our way of life. As social systems become increasingly complex, communication becomes more and more important. Cheap paper is no longer a luxury, it is a positive necessity.

33

We want all of these things but they are not all compatible. They all place a drain on the forests—and the forests are finite. As one area is supported another must be cut back; else we may overstrain•the resource. Scientific advances can tell us how to manage the forests for increasing efficiency, if that is what we choose, but the real problem is to determine just what it is that we want from the forests and what, of that, we can realistically have.

Should clearcutting be prohibited? The answer requires an understanding of clearcutting and its uses. Clearcutting is one tool for forest management; it is one of many methods of harvest. Like any method it has its advantages and disadvantages. Whether it should be used is but one small part of the much larger controversy over how intensely our forests should be used.

That decision depends on our priorities. National priorities for forest use should not just happen. They should be established with a full understanding of the goals which will have to be sacrificed in the process of achieving others. Once social priorities are established it will be a far simpler task to determine scientifically which silvicultural methods will be most helpful in attaining the desired goals.

2

Clearcutting in the Public Forests of the North Central Region

by
Lee M. James
Chairman,
Department of Forestry
Michigan State University

THE PRODUCTION OF TIMBER is one of the basic functions of national forests. This was first established in 1897 by the Organic Act and was noted again in 1911 when land acquisition for a national forest system was authorized. It was re-stated in 1960 by the Multiple-Use Act which notes that forest management is to be directed toward outdoor recreation, range, timber production, watershed protection, and fish and wildlife resources. This is a mandate which indicates clearly the interrelated objectives of forest management and which reaffirms the role of timber production among the functions of the forest. Such is the charge, but public forestry agencies have found that it is extremely difficult to steer a course which recognizes all the interrelated forest values and the legitimate demands of the many different groups of users, for management which attempts to steer a middle course among all concerned user groups most frequently succeeds in satisfying none of them.

BACKGROUND AND A LOOK AHEAD

Originally, forests covered nearly half the land area of the present-day United States. From the Atlantic Coast, forests extended westward in an almost unbroken expanse to the

35

central prairies. West of the Great Plains, forests occurred in more isolated groups. On the West Coast, another solid belt of forest stretched from Alaska to northern California.

Inroads into the original forests for farming, settlement, and timber production were extensive, particularly in the eastern part of the country. Much of the original forest has been altered drastically, while extensive areas formerly cultivated have been abandoned and allowed to revert to forest.

Until well into the twentieth century, forests were exploited and left. The clearing and destruction caused by logging of that era proceeded at a rate which alarmed many. At the beginning of this century, even foresters tended to view clearcutting as bad silvicultural practice. Light partial cutting was held up as the goal in forest management. Such partial cutting became firmly established in eastern hardwood forests. In some forest types, however, experience with partial cutting was not successful. An effort in the 1930's to apply partial cutting to West Coast Douglas fir ended in failure due to deterioration of stands caused by wind, ice and rots, and to replacement of Douglas fir by the more shade-tolerant hemlocks and true firs.

In the eastern spruce types, partial cutting resulted in blowdown of residual trees and replacement of spruce by less valuable species. Partial cutting in Lake States jack pine was a complete failure. Jack pine reproduction failed and the residual trees grew less well than trees in adjoining uncut areas. Clearcutting came to be the preferred method of harvest in these areas.

It is ironic, in the context of current controversies, that efforts to intensify silvicultural practice in recent decades have led foresters to make greater use of clearcutting as a silvicultural tool.

After more than three centuries of settlement and development, forests still occupy 760 million acres—one-third the acreage of the United States. Noncommercial forest comprises 250 million acres of this. Most noncommercial forest is unproductive for timber-growing, but some 16 million acres of otherwise productive forest land have been withdrawn from timber production by law as state parks, national parks and wilderness areas in national forests.

Some 510 million acres are now classified as commercial forest land; three-fourths of this is concentrated in the East. This is land judged to be suitable and available for the growing of continuous crops of industrial timber products. The commercial forest is distributed regionally as follows:

	Million acres
North	176.0
South	198.8
Rocky Mountains	66.1
Pacific Coast	69.3
Total	510.2

Increases have occurred as farm lands have been abandoned to forest, and decreases have accompanied withdrawals for urban development, highways and other uses. The net effect has been an *increase* of about 50 million acres of forest since 1910. Recently the rate of gain in forest area has fallen off, and within the decade, the area of commercial forest can be expected to begin declining.

For several decades, overall timber production was essentially stable, but during the last decade it increased by nearly two billion cubic feet. This raises the question of timber supplies for the future.

In the eastern United States, timber growth exceeds timber cut. In the West, however, the volume cut is considerably larger than the volume grown. There is some question about whether the West can sustain this current level of sawtimber cut indefinitely.

Timber Trends (1965) and other national studies have calculated projected timber needs and prices using a variety of data. All projections point to a future supply problem. If both

37

production and harvest proceed as anticipated, timber supply in the year 2000 is seen as considerably short of all of the demand projections.

Early national policy emphasized transferring public domain lands to private ownership. By the time this policy was abandoned in the late 1800's, most of the productive forest lands were privately owned. Nevertheless a large public forest estate was created out of the remaining lands and its area has been increased by exchanges and purchases during this century. As of 1968, the 510 million acres of commercial forest land were distributed as follows; national forest, 97; other federal lands, 16; state and local, 29; forest industry, 66; farm, 141; and miscellaneous private, 161.

Although the national forests contain only 19 percent of the nation's commercial forest land, strong protection efforts and conservative management have made the public timber increasingly important in terms of volume. The national forests now contain 35 percent of the timber growing stock and 44 percent of the nation's sawtimber resource.

Forest industry has emerged as a major class of ownership. Holding 15 percent of the commercial forest, forest industry has 15 percent of the timber growing stock.

About 28 percent of the commercial forest land is in farms and another 31 percent is in miscellaneous private ownership. These farm and private lands are among the most poorly managed forest lands, yet they supply about half of the timber volume cut in the United States. Timber growth has increased markedly on these lands largely as a consequence of public programs of protection against fire and pests, education, tax incentives, and public assistance programs in timber management and marketing. Nevertheless, non-industrial, private owners as a group have not invested in timber management. Withdrawals of private forest lands for other uses and increasing use of land for housing and recreation suggest that there is little likelihood of much expansion in the timber supply from the non-industrial sector. Increasingly, the burden of sustaining and

38

increasing timber supply has fallen on forest-industry and public lands.

Forest industry, with 67 million acres of commercial forest, currently produces about 3.5 billion cubic feet of timber annually. These industrial forests are more productive on the average than national forest lands and a further intensification of management can be expected. Nevertheless, it is not likely that the forest industry can do more than double its sustained annual output by the year 2000. That is not sufficient to meet the projected needs.

Public forests, then, are left with a major role in supplying current and future timber demands. At present, the public forests account for at least a fourth of the national timber output. Substantial yields of timber may be expected from federal forests even without an increase in the intensity of management. The assumption here is that continuation of the present level of road building will open up some 68 million acres of national forest land by the year 2000. This area will yield 3.6 billion cubic feet as contrasted with 2.7 billion feet realized in 1968. It is a sizeable increase but it is not enough.

Under present management standards, stable price timber demands in the future cannot be met with prospective timber supplies. Extension of available timber supplies may be sought through closer utilization of wood residues now wasted, by increased efficiency in manufacturing wood products, by more efficient design in construction and by increasing re-use of paper and board. Nevertheless, intensified management of forests represents the principal long-range opportunity for supplying expanded timber markets. Although intensification of management may be encouraged on private lands, federal lands remain a primary source of material with which the national demand for timber can be met.

METHODS OF CUTTING

There are many methods of cutting; each has its particular advantages and purposes. Partial cuts create stands of mixed age trees while complete cuts create even-aged stands.

Intermediate cuttings are applied to even-aged stands prior to harvesting for a variety of purposes including cleaning, liberation, thinning and salvage. Cleaning is an operation in a young stand, not past the sapling stage. It liberates trees from competition of trees of similar age but of less desirable species or form. A liberation cutting is also applied at the sapling stage but it removes trees larger and older than the favored trees. An improvement cutting is made after the sapling stage by removing the less desirable trees in the main crown canopy. A thinning is a cutting in an immature stand which increases the growth rate of crop trees, improves composition and promotes sanitation. Salvage cutting is used to remove useable trees killed or damaged by injurious agencies other than competition. All of these are cutting methods used during the rotation while the trees are growing to maturity.

Cutting methods at the end of the rotation in even-aged management are designed to yield a harvest of timber products and to provide for reproduction or regeneration. The methods employed for such harvesting in even-aged stands are clearcutting, seed tree cutting and shelterwood cutting.

Clearcutting refers to the removal of an entire stand in one cut. It may be employed silviculturally to enable the forester to manage establishment, composition and growth of the forest. It should not be confused with the destructive logging practices of the late nineteenth century.

Shelterwood cutting provides for removal of the mature timber in a series of two or more cuttings. Regeneration of the stand begins under a partial forest canopy. A final harvest of the shelterwood removes the cover and permits the new stand to develop as an even-aged one.

The seed tree method fits somewhere between clearcutting and shelterwood. It provides for removal of the mature timber in one cut with a few seed trees left standing to insure the establishment of reproduction.

Only one cutting method, selection, applies to uneven-aged stands. The mature timber is removed either as single scattered

Passing machinery or falling timber may damage trees left standing after selective cutting methods. Such damage permits parasites and diseases to enter otherwise healthy wood and may cause significant economic losses.

42   *A strong healthy tree may, in time grow around and over the site of an old injury, sealing it off from external influences.*

Once rot and insects invade a tree through any injury, the tree is weakened and subject to damage by wind or fire.

trees or in small groups at relatively short intervals repeated indefinitely.

The choice of cutting method in a managed forest is determined by ecological and economic considerations. Choices may be made on the basis of species composition, age of trees, condition of stands, soils, topography, microclimate, economics of harvesting, and objectives of management. All are subject to misapplication, but inherently all methods are compatible with concepts of sustained yield and multiple use.

Economic considerations frequently encourage maintenance of nature's prescription of even-aged management. The most valuable species in any region tend to be relatively intolerant trees growing in even-aged stands. All pines, western larch, and Douglas fir are examples of intolerant softwoods while black walnut, yellow birch, yellow poplar and black cherry are examples of intolerant hardwoods. If not managed under an even-aged system, these valuable intolerant species tend to be followed in ecological succession by slower growing, more tolerant species of lesser value.

If trees are to be planted artificially, making use of genetically superior planting stock, clearcutting is generally the only suitable cutting method to use. Clearcutting also facilitates the disposal of slash and debris; hence it lowers the fire danger.

Some specific ecological factors point to extensive use of clearcutting or other even-aged management methods. A forest composed of large trees of advanced age and declining vigor faces high mortality losses under uneven-aged management. Where dwarf mistletoe is a problem, as it is in many parts of the West, a healthy new stand can be grown only after removal of all the old trees. Periodic burning to reduce the fire hazard in slash pine can be carried out only in even-aged stands. The risk of windfall dictates against uneven-aged management on exposed slopes or in shallow-rooted stands on wet soils.

The principal disadvantage inherent in clearcutting and seed tree methods is the inevitable marring of the scenery following logging. Another criticism is that the even-aged stand does not offer as great resistance to injury from wind, snow, glaze, insects, and disease as does the unevenaged stand. Other disadvantages of even-aged management are usually the result of misapplication or poor judgment; they are not inherent in the system. Among the problems caused by incorrect clearcutting are excessive soil erosion, runoff, and damage to water quality, particularly where large clearcuts have been made on steep slopes.

At the present time, clearcutting accounts for more than half the total volume of wood removed from the national forests annually. Even-aged management is the rule, but clearcutting shares the stage with intermediate, shelterwood and seed tree treatments. Intermediate treatments are used relatively more frequently in eastern forests; shelterwood and seed tree methods are most common in the West.

Independent of the basic merits of clearcutting as a useful cutting practice is the issue of errors in application. Errors have been committed and they have precipitated much of the current controversy. Continuance of errors on some minimal basis must be assumed, but one must guard against the more obvious errors which have been committed: poor road design and maintenance resulting in excess runoff and erosion; insensitivity to design factors in size, shape and location of clearcuts; clearcutting on sites subject to erosion damage; clearcutting on sites where successful regeneration cannot be anticipated; and clearcutting in areas with dubious sustained yield capabilities.

ECONOMICS

For economic reasons too, foresters favor clearcutting. Those species which are the most desirable for commercial purposes— southern pines, Douglas fir, yellow poplar, black walnut, black cherry and red oak—are intolerant and give way to other species in the natural progression of growth. If even-aged management were abandoned on public forests and replaced by uneven-aged management, an economic loss would be involved in the

45

transition of species. A related economic loss involved in any transition from intolerant to tolerant species caused by a drastic change in cutting methods would be a marked decline in the sustainable annual cut of timber.

Under even-aged management, the permanent road system need not be built as rapidly and the temporary road system need not be as extensive as under uneven-aged management, because the annual yield of a forest can be obtained from a more concentrated area. Logging costs in general are lower under even-aged management because of the large volume of timber removed per unit area and because of fewer constraints on the use of efficient machines. Administration, too, is less costly and simpler than it is under a selection system. Many stands now operable under even-aged management would become submarginal if the additional costs of logging by selection had to be absorbed.

An additional effect of any massive increase in private timber supply caused by curtailment of cutting on federal lands would be a great increase in the extent of clearcutting on private lands and a likely increase in damaging environmental impacts.

IMPACTS OF CLEARCUTTING

Esthetics—The scarring of the forest by logging, however temporary, is disturbing to most observers. The most careful planning for visual effects is needed in clearcutting. Road construction also has an esthetic impact and design is needed to avoid emphasizing the straight-line appearance of the clearcut. Also, site preparation for reforestation is unattractive. In situations where visual effects are important, shelterwood cutting should be considered the preferred method of even-aged management insofar as it is a technically acceptable alternative.

Recreation—The relation between timber harvesting and recreation depends strongly on the type of recreation and the timing of the cutting. Wilderness users require the absence of all cutting for their recreation. Skiers require clearcutting in the areas of greatest interest to them. Mass recreation requires simply that evidence of logging be minimal and that it should avoid areas of special interest. A crucial point to note is that annual harvest affects only a small part of the managed forest. Recreation users concentrate on the areas that attract them most and avoid areas lacking attraction. If cutting is avoided on all sites where the establishment of new forest is questionable, the impact of harvesting on recreation use may be very slight. In Western Europe and Japan, forests have been managed for centuries under clearcutting systems and are heavily used for recreation.

Wildlife—Openings in the forest stimulate the development of young trees, shrubs and herbaceous plants needed by many animals. No one stand condition can be generalized as the most desirable for wildlife management but there is a strong case for clearcutting. In lower Michigan, clearcutting has been shown to double the pounds of deer browse produced. Similar results have been reported for the central Rockies and the South. Wild turkeys, smaller game birds and songbirds seek openings created by clearcutting for warmth as well as for feeding and nesting. They turn to the adjacent uncut stands for shelter. A great deal still needs to be learned about the details of cutting and their effects, but the indication is strong that even-aged stand management, usually with clearcutting, is generally more productive for wildlife than uneven-aged stand management.

Fish—Temperature of streams is a key factor in trout survival. Brook trout, for example, rarely occur in waters in which summer temperatures exceed 68°F. Cutting close to a stream removes protective cover and thus may have an adverse effect on trout by increasing water temperature. The more complete the cutting, the more intense the effect. For this reason clearcutting near streams should be avoided.

Water—In a closed forest, much of the precipitation never reaches the ground; it is intercepted by the canopy and evaporates. Moisture which does reach the ground is absorbed by the humus which acts as a great sponge. Cutting reduces the direct water losses—those due to interception, evaporation and transpiration—but it increases losses due to runoff, so that streamflow is greater and occasional flooding may occur.

If the ground is frozen or saturated, overland flows from rains or melting snows will produce flooding regardless of the cutting treatment used or even the absence of cutting. A forest floor open to percolation is unlikely to support overland flows even after clearcutting so long as litter and humus layers remain intact. When flooding does occur it is frequently the result of snowmelt in the early spring. If peak flows from tributaries coincide to produce a flood peak in a major stream, clearcutting may actually ease the situation by accelerating runoff from the cut areas.

Such effects, good and bad, are of short duration, however, as vegetation becomes re-established and the effects diminish rapidly. Within ten years the effects may become completely negligible.

In terms of preventing soil erosion, the forest is, of course, at its best in undisturbed condition. To approximate this state, care is needed in the construction and maintenance of logging roads and in the diversion of road wash through filtering areas before the water reaches any stream course.

Nutrients—Trees accumulate sizable amounts of nutrients in stems, branches, roots, leaves and fruits but the total amount is a small fraction of that which is available in the forest floor and soil mantle. Nutrients are constantly added to this system from the atmosphere and from decomposition of leaves. Needles and debris left on the ground after logging contain a larger amount of nutrients than do the logs. Thus log removal does not cause serious loss of nutrients from the forest.

More significant nutrient losses are likely to be losses in runoff water from the forest floor and soil rather than in wood removed. Highly podzolized soils found in the Northeast appear to be more susceptible to such nutrient losses after timber cutting than other soils. In general, however, research has shown these losses to be small enough and of short enough duration to be acceptable for most soils.

IMPACT ON VARIED FOREST TYPES

The White-Red-Jack Pine Group—This group includes those boreal and northern forest cover types in which any of the named trees plays a dominant role.

Jack pine is a very intolerant species, almost always occurring in fairly pure even-aged stands. On dry sites it forms an edaphic climax while on sites with more moisture and nutrients, it tends to be replaced by red pine, white pine or the more tolerant hardwoods. Maturity is reached in 50 years on poor sites and in up to 100 years on good ones. At maturity and after, the trees are highly susceptible to wind damage and windthrow. Despite the fact that jack pine has, by now, been regenerated successfully under an overstory which was later clearcut, jack pine is still known as a "fire species" as it does need *full* sunlight for best development.

Because of its intolerance and because of harvesting costs, mature jack pine stands are usually clearcut. This has been the prescription and almost exclusive practice for over 25 years. The soil is scarified to stimulate regeneration, and cone-bearing slash is scattered over the bared surface where higher air temperatures near the ground open the cones and release their seeds.

Red pine, too, is intolerant but it is far less so than jack pine. On moist sites this species gradually gives way to aspen or to the more tolerant hardwoods. Selection cannot be used with this species. Brush readily invades stands which are not dense, making it difficult to regenerate them to red pine. To avoid this, mature stands must be cut drastically; they are usually harvested by the shelterwood method.

White pine, the most important commercial species of the three, is found primarily in second growth stands, much of it in mixture with various hardwoods. This species occurs on sites having a wider range of moisture and nutrient levels than either jack or red pine. Because white pine grows under such a variety of conditions, there are no uniform silvicultural recommendations. Generally, even-aged management appears most applicable, with the shelterwood methods used for harvesting mature stands, but clearcutting followed by planting also appears to have considerable application in white pine silviculture.

Specific data on the impact of various cutting practices used for this pine group on the watershed values are not available. Relatively few areas occupied by the pines, however, are in areas where watershed values are critical, so that the impact may be expected to be of low importance.

Many studies have shown that clearcutting brings about highly desirable food and cover conditions for many wildlife species. One study of the pine region in New Jersey showed that the area could indeed produce both deer and timber under a program of balanced forest and wildlife management. Ruffed grouse also have been the subject of study. They frequent the pine forests and even-aged management with clearcutting has been found to provide desirable habitat for them.

Clearcutting in jack pine is a necessary part of the habitat management program for the Kirtland's warbler in Michigan. This warbler nests on the ground in stands of jack pine which cover at least 80 acres, in which trees are six to 18 feet tall and have living lower branches which reach down to dense ground cover. Management for the Kirtland's warbler includes the removal of old timber by clearcutting, followed by burning to regenerate the jack pine on about one square mile every few years.

In jack pine, a two-cut shelterwood method applied in Michigan proved that clearcutting was not the only possible harvest method, as adequate regeneration was established in seven to 10 years after the seed cutting. This method of harvest enhanced wildlife habitat conditions and provided more variable vegetational stages yielding food and cover than were obtained by clearcutting. Esthetically, the shelterwood method appears to be more acceptable than clearcutting as the stand is reestablished before the overstory is removed completely. Shelterwood may prove increasingly applicable in jack pine; it is also highly satisfactory in red and white pine types.

The Spruce-Fir Group—The tree types in this group are most prevalent on sites which are excessively wet and which are poorly aerated because of poor drainage or because of an excess of precipitation over evaporation. In the Lake States this is primarily a lowland association composed of black spruce, tamarack, northern white cedar, balsam fir, balsam poplar, black ash and red maple. An upland form of this type found more commonly in the Northeast consists of mixtures of white spruce, balsam fir, paper birch and aspen, or red spruce, balsam fir, red maple, hemlock and yellow birch. Composition of the stands is highly varied as is the nature of the growing sites. The wide variation in spruce-fir-hardwood sites is matched by an equally wide range in growth rates.

Certain stands and species pose special problems to the forester. Stands of low production such as those found on the thin-soiled upper slopes of northeastern forests are distinctly marginal and are best left uncut. Balsam fir is highly susceptible to butt rot and subsequent wind breakage after the trees reach 60 years of age. Management of stands with considerable balsam fir must always be influenced strongly by such pathological considerations.

Clearcutting is essential in spruce-fir to obtain the maximum value of wood products which the sites occupied by this group can produce. The most important losses to be avoided are those caused by wind. This can be accomplished by keeping stands as dense as possible, even where some thinning must be applied,

51

and harvesting the mature stand by clearcutting. In the absence of clearcutting, the fir component will increase at the expense of the more desirable spruce, and other less desirable species such as red maple will also increase in numbers.

Sites occupied by spruce-fir stands are often important watershed areas because of their generally moist or wet condition and their significant contribution to stream flow. Where snow accounts for much of the precipitation, clearcutting can increase the water yield from streamflow. Extra snow deposited on clearcut strips yields more water to streamflow than does snow from uncut areas due to a faster melting in clearcut areas and a smaller water deficit in the soil mantle from lower evapo-transpiration loss in the summer.

As in the case with other forest types, this association, when it is clearcut, gives way to food and cover types desirable for deer and possibly other forms of wildlife. However, recreationists in the Superior National Forest list *fishing* as a major attraction, with high priority also given to the wilderness aspects of the area. In view of this, any clearcutting within sight of areas used by recreationists in this forest would be generally undesirable.

One major concern practically eliminates consideration of cutting methods other than clearcutting for swamp conifers. Growing as they do on wet, poorly drained sites, they are shallow rooted and highly subject to windthrow. Thus, partial cutting of any kind tends to open up the stand to severe losses from blowdown. The clearcuttings, however, need not be in large blocks. Narrow strip or patch cuttings are actually preferable. Shelterwood cutting is an acceptable alternative on sites where the stands are fairly windfirm. Spruce-fir stands which are uneven-aged, or which should not be managed by even-aged methods for esthetic or other reasons, can be given a periodic selection cutting to maintain the uneven-aged stand form. In such cases, however, less desirable and slower growing tolerant hardwoods will increase, thus lowering production of the stand, and also usually the value of the timber produced.

52

The Oak-Hickory Group—East of the Great Plains, oak-hickory forests dominate the forest landscape. Major species in this group are white, black, and red oaks and several species of hickories. Important associated species are elm, basswood, walnut, beech, sugar maple, yellow poplar, ash, and pine.

Early cuttings in the oak-hickory forests removed only the high quality oaks, black walnut, yellow poplar, black cherry and other select species. Residual stands thus became culled remnants of the old-growth forests. Fire has added to the cull problem in the stands as has grazing by livestock.

In general, even-aged management is recommended for maximum production of the highest quality material of the most preferred species. On the best sites, sawtimber and veneer logs can be produced on rotations of 60 to 75 years. Periodic thinnings and improvement cuttings are justified prior to harvest clearcutting. The best new stems of oak and hickory for the regenerated stand come from advance reproduction which was cut or broken in the logging operation and resprouts.

On medium sites, several intermediate cuttings need to be applied to increase the quality and value of the mature stand. The stands are clearcut at maturity.

On poor sites, the oak-hickory stand may be managed for pulpwood. Very little cultural work can be justified on these sites; they should be regarded as protection forests. When such an area yields a commercial harvest, total removal of the mature stand by clearcutting is recommended. In some cases, conversion to pine on these sites may be justified.

Most research efforts in the past 30 years have reached the same general conclusions regarding management of the oak-hickory forests—they should be grown in even-aged stands, and they should be regenerated by clearcutting.

Most ungrazed, well stocked oak-hickory stands have ample advance reproduction when stands are mature. The removal of the entire stand thus stimulates successful regeneration while cutting of small openings will not do so.

53

A serious problem in oak-hickory management is that trees in the residual stand will develop profuse epicormic branching following release by selection or shelterwood cuttings. In clearcutting, border trees will also produce epicormic branching so that log quality is lowered. Thus the amount of degradation in a stand is directly related to the total length of the opening border. As circular openings have less border than square openings, which in turn have less border than rectangular ones, an attempt should be made to cut openings as large as is consistent with other silvicultural and management objectives.

Several watershed areas in the oak-hickory forests have been under study both before and after clearcutting treatment. Findings show that there is considerable impact of clearcutting on watershed conditions, that the effects are short term and that they may be either beneficial by increasing streamflow, or somewhat detrimental by temporarily increasing turbidity in run-off water, primarily from improperly placed logging roads.

Forests of this type provide essential habitat for white-tailed deer and other wildlife species throughout the range. Within these forests, clearcutting has been shown to cause high levels of browse production which may last, in a clearcut area, for as long as 20 or 30 years. Clearcuttings in the oak-hickory forest also provide the brushy condition which is heavily used for cover by non-yarding deer.

Some low grade oak-hickory stands on poor sites might properly be managed specifically for browse by patch bulldozing. In lower Michigan, a bulldozer was used to push over all trees on a small area. Five years after bulldozing, many of the pushed-over trees were still alive because their roots were still partially attached and were producing browse in their prostrate crowns and numerous epicormic branches.

Clearcutting which causes organic sediments to be carried into trout streams can cause damage to fish habitat. This effect is critical in streams with high temperatures because the decomposition further reduces an already low supply of oxygen. Sediments cover bottom fauna and trout eggs. They

54

reduce water transparency and thus the light available for the growth of green plants. In a marginal stream, a change of a few degrees accompanying such alteration might eliminate the trout population altogether.

Most people find a mature stand of timber esthetically pleasing. The loss of such a stand, together with the appearance of devastation left immediately after a clearcutting, are strongly objectionable. This is especially important in the oak-hickory forests located close to population centers where access is easy and public use of the forest is heavy.

There are alternatives to clearcutting as prompt regeneration in oak-hickory forests can usually be obtained with any silvicultural method. However, research efforts comparing results of clearcutting with those following other cutting methods show that the other methods result in less desirable stand composition and stand quality than clearcutting. Obviously selection cutting is far more acceptable than clearcutting from a recreational and esthetic standpoint, so that on balance, shelterwood cutting, a compromise, is probably somewhat preferable to clearcutting.

The Elm-Ash-Cottonwood Group—Elm, ash, red maple and cottonwoods are characteristic of forest types which occur throughout the North Central region along water courses and on soils with a high water table or poor internal drainage. Yellow poplar, northern red oak and many other moist-site upland species often join the basic types on the better drained areas. Since these soils are highly productive for agriculture, clearing and drainage for such use have reduced and are continuing to reduce the area of this type.

Cottonwood is especially important as a pioneer species on these sites. As it is highly intolerant, it is gradually eliminated from its natural sites in the absence of cutting or natural catastrophe. Elm and maple, on the other hand, are tolerant and are generally climax species for the sites occupied. Elm, however, is disappearing from the association because of Dutch

55

elm disease. As the elms die off, the more tolerant species of this group are expanding into its erstwhile growing space.

Elm-ash-cottonwood stands are generally managed under an even-aged regime with clearcutting applied at maturity, followed by a program to control undesirable species such as box elder and privet. Cottonwood is difficult to establish from seed so it is often established by planting cuttings.

On favorable sites, especially those having a high proportion of cottonwoods, thinning should be applied to promote growth of the best trees.

Once cutting has been initiated on sites occupied by this group, there is a problem of invasion by brush, willows and other undesirables such as box elder which grow up quickly. Such invasion is less successful however, with the total disturbance accompanying clearcutting than it is with other cutting methods.

The elm-ash-cottonwood type is concentrated in wet areas; hence, it is reasonable to expect that increases in water yields following logging on these sites would be greater than they would for other types on drier sites. The sites are wet and thus they have more water to give up to streamflow.

Areas occupied by this forest type are frequently used for dispersed recreation such as hunting or fishing. Hunters and fishermen occasionally take objection, on an esthetic basis, to logging but their major objection is to the dense tangle of seedlings, sprouts and herbaceous vegetation which comes up so readily on these sites for a few years immediately following logging.

In this association, there is no good alternative to clearcutting. Application of the shelterwood method or selection cuttings will reduce or even eliminate the fast-growing, intolerant cottonwood. The slower growing ash, elm, and associated species will replace the cottonwood and invasion by box elder and privet may occur. Thus total timber production will be significantly reduced if clearcutting is not used.

The Aspen-Paper Birch Group—Aspen and paper birch occur in pure stands or in varying degrees of mixture with each other. Many silvical characteristics of the species are so similar and management procedures are so nearly identical, that the aspen-birch group can be treated as basically one type. The type occurs on the full range of site conditions from clays to sands, and from moist to dry.

Aspen is intolerant and paper birch is only slightly less so. The success of aspen is due almost entirely to its tremendous capacity to produce root suckers and to grow quickly in taking over cutover or burnt areas. Paper birch too is an aggressive species, becoming established wherever mineral soil has been exposed. Such exposure is usually due to fires or logging and without such disturbances aspen and paper birch are minor components in many forest types. Heinselman has predicted that by 1990, one-third, or nearly six million acres of this type, will convert naturally to other species, mostly northern hardwoods and spruce-fir. This may have its economic advantages as some of the pines, spruce and hardwoods which will take over the aspen and birch stands are in fact more valuable.

The intolerance of the species and the even-aged stand form require that clearcutting be applied at rotation age to reestablish aspen and paper birch. In addition, one must consider defense against the most serious disease of aspen, hypoxylon canker. To minimize losses to this disease, stands should not be thinned or partially cut. They should be allowed to grow at the greatest possible density and then harvested and regenerated by clearcutting.

Recreational and esthetic concerns are particularly important in cutting paper birch, because it is among the most attractive and beautiful species in this country. Thus, decisions on the type of harvest cuts to be made in stands containing paper birch are often dictated by considerations other than birch reproduction. Management for esthetic purposes requires cultural measures and schedules different from those employed for

57

timber production. Appearance is important, not maximum growth, and stump sprouts are highly desirable as birch clumps are especially attractive.

Any cutting treatment other than complete clearcutting (or no cutting) will be detrimental to aspen-birch reproduction. Both are intolerant and yield easily in successional trend to a wide variety of more tolerant species. Both types are highly attractive and so, for aesthetic reasons, the minimum ecological requirement for their maintenance is small patch clearcutting. If conversion to conifers or tolerant hardwoods is an acceptable consequence of management, then any cutting method short of clearcutting is a reasonable alternative.

The Northern Hardwoods Group—The sugarmaple—beech—yellow birch type is the backbone of the northern hardwoods group. Many other types and associations are recognized but the transition between them is often indefinite and their reaction to treatment is so similar that they are usually grouped together for discussion purposes.

Most northern hardwoods are second-growth stands that arose after commercial clearcutting. They are usually well stocked with saplings, poles and small sawtimber. Stand quality is variable and the stands are usually uneven-aged.

Most species in the northern hardwoods are tolerant so that the group is definitely a climax association, one which aggressively recaptures a site after logging. During the first year after logging, water yield on such cutover watershed areas increases by four to 12 inches. The increase is most noticable in the late summer months. Rapid regrowth reduces the extra water yield and by 10 years after logging the increase has disappeared.

Dispersed recreation may be enhanced by judicious, limited clearcutting in northern hardwoods by providing contrasts in forest cover and scenery for the hiker and casual forest viewer. Clearcutting is of course incompatible with concentrated recreational use. Fortunately, however, northern hardwoods are

A healthy young stand of aspen grows vigorously on this land which was clear-cut four years before. Photo, Michigan State University

tolerant species so selection cuttings can be applied near concentrated recreational areas if cutting of any kind is considered necessary.

Selection silviculture has generally been recommended and applied in northern hardwoods. That this is the best management procedure is still the view of most forest managers in the Lake States region. In contrast, Northeastern foresters are becoming increasingly convinced that selection cutting of these hardwoods is a "sacred cow." They advocate even-aged management including clearcutting for maximizing benefits from northern hardwoods. Perhaps the strongest argument in favor of even-aged management is the serious logging damage suffered by the residual stand during partial cutting operations.

In summary, the northern hardwood type is without a doubt the most versatile of our important forest components. It can be managed fairly successfully by selection, shelterwood or clearcutting methods, depending on specific management objectives and local circumstances. The weight of evidence for most objectives appears to be in favor of even-aged management procedures, but these do not necessarily need to be accomplished by clearcutting—the shelterwood method is, in general, an acceptable alternative. Where this is not the case, the selection method can be applied, with the recognition that consequences such as species change and changed operating economics can be expected.

POLICY RECOMMENDATIONS

The Forest Service and the Bureau of Land Management (BLM), major agencies in timber production, are guided by sustained yield principles in timber production, multiple uses of lands and constraints of the Environmental Quality Act of 1969. They have eliminated or restricted timber harvesting in areas recognized as having other and special uses but, in general, they have assumed timber production to be their primary goal and the aim of their management. This assumption is based on mandates and

60

needs discussed earlier. The timber production responsibilities have been buttressed by federal budget guidelines and by professional judgment within the managing agencies so that timber production can be pursued with little loss to other values.

The significant role of federal lands in timber production needs definition and clarification. Without abandoning the concept of overall multiple use, the Congress should require that federal forest lands be classified as to primary use. Under this concept, highly productive forest lands which are not uniquely valuable for other uses would be classified as primarily timberlands. Other areas would be assigned to other primary uses.

This classification of federal lands should be done under the direction of an independent commission broadly based to represent all uses of federal lands. Such an approach would provide a basis for public land management which would help minimize agency dilemmas in deciding on public land use and which would lead to more efficient management practices.

Primary timberland classification would still require sustained-yield production and concern for avoiding unfavorable environmental effects, and it would permit other land uses insofar as they do not conflict with the primary objective.

However, the air would be cleared in important ways. The classification decisions would be arrived at through a process involving broad agency and public participation under an independent commission and requiring congressional approval.

In primary timberlands cutting practices would be determined by economics and ecological requirements of forest stands with the managing agency being free to follow whatever cutting methods it deemed best. Timber management would not be excluded from lands classified for other primary uses, but its secondary position would be made clear. In such areas, the managing agency would have to defend cutting on the basis that it was being used as a tool to enhance the primary value of the area.

Evaluation of cutting methods in this report makes it clear that carefully designed clearcuts are generally the most appropriate in terms of maximizing timber productivity and wildlife habitat and minimizing utilization costs. Clearcutting does, however, have an unfortunate effect on the general public in esthetic impact. It may have other harmful effects, usually due to mistakes in managerial judgment or overzealous devotion to timber production.

3 | Clearcutting in the Hardwood Forests of the Northeast

by
W. W. Ward
Director
School of Forest Resources
Pennsylvania State University

CLEARCUTTING IN THE HARDWOOD FORESTS of the Northeast has been practiced continuously since colonization. There are relatively few acres of existing forest areas that have not been clearcut at least once, and most of them have been clearcut two or more times. The oak-hickory forests of Pennsylvania, for example, were clearcut for charcoal two or three times during the nineteenth century. As coke replaced wood charcoal in the smelters, the iron companies sold these areas to the state. Similarly, many portions of the present Allegheny National Forest were cut over twice; once for timber and once for chemical wood. Starting in 1911 many such areas in the Northeast were purchased as national forest lands. Since these forests had been clearcut, it was obvious to both the sellers and the buyers that future harvest operations could not be expected for about 40 to 100 years. The sellers were aware of the loss of the charcoal market; they could not anticipate the development of the pulp and paper market, nor the great future demand for hardwood lumber. To restore the areas, public foresters correctly interpreted their prime mission as one of fire protection in the young stands. This goal they pursued with phenomenal success.

As the stands grew into the 40-60 year age class it was apparent that many trees of poor form and condition prevented the proper development of more desirable individuals in the

63

dense stands. Improvement cutting and thinning were obviously in order. Where markets existed for pulpwood, lumber or small timber, the trees to be weeded out could be sold to a commercial operator, particularly if a large volume was to be removed and if low-cost logging was convenient. Where these conditions did not exist, stands remained crowded and unimproved. With the meager funds available, men were employed to girdle or fell undesirable trees in the unthinned areas. The intention of this effort was to increase the quality of growth in the trees remaining in these "middle-aged" stands.

Terms like "selection cutting" and "partial cutting" have been applied to these thinning operations. Unfortunately, many laymen and even a few professionals fail to note that these treatments were means to an end—the eventual harvest—and were not ends in themselves. Sooner or later the crop will be harvested, either by man or by nature, and a new crop will be initiated. Fortunately forest stands have a more flexible end period than do fields of corn or crops of apples; this is the encouraging part of the present dilemma of when and how to harvest.

Many of the older stands on the national and state forests of the Northeast are now mature; others are rapidly approaching that age. Many people would prefer to have the present stands remain forever as they are now, but they won't. The forest is a dynamic community and change is inevitable. Its uses, whatever the priorities determined, must be planned. Timber values may not seem as important now as they once were, but they remain high. Harvest must be planned many years ahead. To rely for products and services only upon mature and near-mature stands as they exist at present is to build-in serious planning problems for the future.

PRESENT STATUS

The total forested area of the New England and Mid-Atlantic States as measured in 1965 was about 75 million acres. This

64

An even-aged stand such as this one in the eastern hardwood forest shows a real dearth of understory vegetation. This stand is about 130 years old and not under management. The factors which caused the even-aged condition here are unknown.

represents nearly 60 percent of the total land area of the region. Most of these lands are privately owned with public forests making up less than 10 percent of all forest land.

Small as they are, the public forests of the area are representative of the forest as a whole. They have the preponderance of their stands in the middle and near-mature age classes some 40 to 80 years old. This figure must be considered in light of the fact that the rotation time for the hardwood forest is 100 years, plus or minus 20 years. This means that by about age 100 the trees will have achieved most of their growth in value and that the rate of increase in value after this point will decrease. At the same time the incidence of disease and other risks will increase.

These forests are not, at present, being pressed for production. The northeastern hardwood forests produce between four and seven times the volume of wood which is being harvested.

The impact of silvicultural clearcutting on the hardwood forests of the Northeast can be evaluated only within a framework of realistic assumptions. At this time, available data suggest that the following assumptions are reasonable; (1) that the proportion of forest land clearcut annually is no more than 1 percent; (2) that the maximum size of an individual clearcut is 100 acres; (3) that the rate of regrowth on cutover areas is rapid, and (4) that partial cuttings have such a small effect that their impact can be ignored. Within this framework it is possible to begin to assess the impact of modern clearcutting on a variety of conditions.

Climate—Obviously the removal of cover over an extended area changes conditions within that area. After a cut, solar radiation is more direct, thus temperature fluctuations are more severe. This affects conditions during the period of initial regrowth. Ground level wind patterns would be altered. The exact nature of the change would depend largely on the size of the clearcut. Wind turbulence would increase at the boundary of the cut area more than at the center. Other climatic changes would have their greatest effect at the center and would diminish toward the boundaries. In any case, changes would be limited to the specific area of the clearcut; there would be little climatic impact beyond the logged area.

Site—The impact of clearcutting appears to be highly dependent on the initial quality of the site. In general eastern hardwood forests which have been clearcut have regenerated rapidly, within less than 10 years. However, where sites are poor, regrowth is slower and any additional environmental stress such as drought, repeated fires, or heavy browsing by deer, could cause plants other than trees to become dominant. Furthermore the understory on poor sites is often composed of woody shrubs. These shrubs present more of a threat to tree regeneration than do the herbaceous species which are characteristic of better sites.

Position on the slope is important in determining the cut's impact. Soils of ridgetops and upper slopes are derived from sandstones and quartzites and are generally shallow. They are low in nutrients and are often deficient in water-holding capacity. The soils of the lower slopes and valleys have derived from shales and limestones. They are deeper, more fertile and have generally better moisture properties. South and west facing slopes are more subject to intense solar radiation during hot periods than are north and east facing slopes. This too affects the moisture properties of the soils. For these reasons the effects of any type of cutting tend to be longer lasting on the poorer sites—the ridges, upper slopes and south and west facing slopes.

Soils—Clearcutting may have both beneficial and detrimental effects on the soil. By eliminating the shading effect of the forest canopy, clearcutting lets the surface soil dry out and warm up more rapidly. This in turn causes more rapid decay of the organic layer, an effect which is desirable in most of the

podzol soils of the northern part of the region. In such soils a large portion of the nutrients present are in fact contained in thick layers of raw humus, in a form unavailable to plants.

Clearcutting also reduces the interception of precipitation allowing more water to reach the ground. The removal of vegetation reduces the loss of soil moisture caused by transpiration. The net result of all this is that beneath the topmost layers, more moisture is available after a clearcut than before. Although this change is temporary, the increased availability of moisture improves growing conditions on medium to dry sites. On poorly drained soils this increase in moisture may present some difficulties. Such poorly drained sites, which make up a very small fraction of the northeastern hardwood forest region, should not be clearcut.

Erosion occurs, when it does, mostly as a consequence of poor logging road layout and maintenance. This problem is independent of the type of cutting being done. Studies indicate that with proper planning and supervision erosion from logging roads should not be serious even in steep mountainous regions. Improperly handled, severe erosion can occur with either clearcutting or partial cutting. Such erosion is more visible, however, after a clearcut.

Temperature—Removal of the forest canopy by clearcutting results in greater temperature extremes at and near the soil surface than are found in the shade of the trees. Under certain conditions of weather, soil, and topography, surface temperatures can be reached which are lethal to newly-germinated seedlings. However, the hardwood species are vigorous sprouters, and the sprouts would seldom be killed by high temperatures. In fact the sprouting of many root-suckering species, such as aspen, is enhanced by high temperatures. Furthermore, the slash left over the area would probably provide sufficient shade for most seedlings to become established. Mortality due to low temperatures is probably of minor

69

A logging road through a selectively cut area may well leave an unsightly scar as does this one in West Virginia. From a distance such a scar is not noticeable but its impact may be profound.

importance although the possible formation of frost pockets should be considered in any silvicultural plan.

Watershed—It is generally accepted that there is a beneficial relationship between forests and streamflow. Forest cover protects the soil from erosion and stabilizes the area, it prevents overland flow, reduces flood peaks, and has a general moderating effect on the streamflow regimen. On the other hand, forests consume large amounts of water which, by transpiration, are lost back to the atmosphere.

Clearcutting of a forested watershed will increase the annual water yield noticeably for the first few years after the cut. Most of this extra flow occurs in summer and during early fall—the growing season. This is the time of year when streamflow is normally lowest and water demands are high.

When clearcutting affects water yield during the October-March period it does so by allowing snow to melt sooner in the exposed areas than beneath the trees. In this way the snowmelt is desynchronized and spread over a longer period of time. The result is reduced danger of flooding caused by rapid snowpack melting and it is this which has traditionally been responsible for many of the damaging late spring floods in the Northeast.

Water Quality—If clearcuts are carried out without appropriate protection of waterways, large sections of streams which previously had been shaded may be exposed to direct sunlight. The resulting rise in temperature speeds up the decay process and may even change the character of the stream from that of a coldwater, trout community to a warm water community, lower in oxygen and considered less desirable for fishing purposes.

There is also evidence that clearcutting temporarily increases mineral and nutrient losses through streamflow from the watershed. The most mobile of the mineral elements is nitrogen which is a key nutrient in tree growth. In fact the total amount of undissolved inorganic material removed by streamflow during

70

Sprouts and seedlings provide good winter browse for deer which frequent recently cutover areas.
Photo, W. W. Ward

the first year or two from a clearcut area may be many times greater than that from an undisturbed watershed. These nutrients, leached from the soil, together with the raised stream temperatures, increase the rate of eutrophication in the stream and may give rise to heavy algal growths. Although these effects are temporary, they bear additional investigation.

Wildlife—Clearcutting can be favorable to nearly all species of wildlife. However for the clearcut to be beneficial, the timing, size and location of the clearcuts is of critical importance. With proper planning clearcutting may increase the carrying capacity of a given portion of range or it may increase the winter food supply for animals of many species.

To be favorable to wildlife, clearcuts must not be too large. Most wildlife species benefit primarily from the extra "edges" produced where the forest meets open lands. Clearcutting in small patches increases the amount of edge per unit area while it stimulates the growth of desirable food and cover plants.

The practice is, of course, unfavorable to animals of the "pristine forest." Clearing as practiced in the early days of the northeastern settlement coupled with fires, land development and market hunting, contributed to the reduction and elimination of many species, among them moose, bison, elk, wolf, mountain lion, lynx, wolverine, fisher, pine marten and passenger pigeon. Today, the special needs of these animals must be considered and where they remain they should be afforded special protective consideration in any forest management plan.

For other animal species, the clearcut encourages plants typical of the early stage of forest succession and thereby provides an increased source of food and cover. It produces a greater variety of plant species and thus it produces a greater degree of ecological stability in some areas.

For 10 to 20 years following a clearcutting operation, deer populations increase noticeably. Other animals, among them

72

ruffed grouse and snowshoe hare, also benefit from the new clearing.

Between 20 and 50 years after the clearcut, conditions in the forest are poor for wildlife. Both forage and cover are sparse as a result of the dense overstory. This is a period of low wildlife values associated with poletimber stands.

From age 50 to the end of the rotation, mast and fruits are produced in quantity. Deer, bear, wild turkeys, grouse and gray squirrels utilize the fruits and the area is once again inviting to wildlife.

Rangeland—Grazing in eastern deciduous forests by domestic animals is incompatible with the objectives of forest management. In some areas non-domestic "grazers" may pose a problem. Occasionally deer populations are so high that their browsing habits may seriously impair or even halt regrowth of the new forest. To ensure regeneration in areas with excessive deer populations, clearcuts must be made large enough up to the 100 acre maximum that deer, even though attracted to the young browse, will be unable to suppress the growth of seedlings. In some cases it has even proved necessary to impede deer access to cut areas by leaving tree tops, intact, scattered over the ground.

Recreation—Because the northeastern forests are close to many urban centers, they are subject to very heavy recreational demands. No doubt clearcutting is incompatible with many permanent recreational developments. Clearcutting could not be considered between ski trails or around picnic and camping areas. Clearcutting can, however, be practiced in the vicinity of picnic and camping areas provided that these areas are thoroughly screened by trees. A clearcut within walking distance could actually enhance the value of the area to recreationists as it would offer visitors an opportunity to see plants and animals which are not found in the uncut forest. The plant species thus favored are frequently the ones which show

73

the most attractive fall colors. Variety might be added to hiking trails if they passed (with explanations) near areas in which improvement practices were being conducted. The clearcut might even serve as an extra source of firewood—a commodity which is always in short supply around older camping developments.

Esthetics—Probably the greatest impact of clearcutting on the recreationist is the visual impact of the new clearcut. Piles of slash, scraggly small trees and large, deformed trees on the site leave a picture of devastation. Although beauty may be present on a small scale within the clearcut, it is often overwhelmed by the large-scale effect. Despite this there are, perhaps, a few redeeming features as vistas are created and wildlife is more readily seen. Both the impression of devastation and the vistas are short-lived, however, as the vegetative regrowth usually takes place rapidly.

Clearcutting is especially undesirable when it is done within an area encompassed by a panoramic view. Even after regrowth has hidden the slash piles, logging roads may appear as scars from a distance and the boundaries of the clearcut remain evident. If many clearcuts were made in the same area the resultant panorama might actually take on a checkerboard appearance which would be anything but esthetically pleasing.

SOME WORDS OF CAUTION

No form of harvest is without hazards. Clearcuts, as any form of tree harvest, must be planned with care. The major objection to clearcutting has been based on esthetic grounds, for a clearcut is not attractive in its earliest stages.

More serious charges have been levelled at the practice from the standpoint of site degradation. The effects of clearcutting are unquestionably more pronounced and more visible on poor sites than on more productive and protected areas. Where a site is very poor, subsequent growth may not even lead to reforestation. Such sites should be identified and clearcutting

Ten years after a clearcut, the young hardwood trees at the right of this road stand 10-20 feet high and provide an attractive stand of young growth in the middle of an older area.

should not be used on them. Neither should clearcutting be used on poorly drained soils where increased soil moisture after a clearcut may cause aeration problems and possibly even lead to standing water.

Surface temperature extremes caused by the removal of cover must be considered both from the standpoint of excessively high temperatures and the possible formation of frost pockets.

The effects of clearcutting on stream quality must also be considered. The rise in stream temperature speeds decay and causes notable changes in the biota of the stream. This may affect the recreational potential of the stream. Where clearcuts are kept small and the stream edge avoided, this should present no problem.

Ecological damage caused by poor road layout and maintenance is a serious problem but it is not one limited to clearcuts. Problems concerning logging roads are the same for all methods of harvest; under clearcut conditions they are merely more apparent than when hidden in a partial cut.

SUMMARY

Clearcutting in the hardwood forests of the Northeast is both biologically and economically a desirable timber producing practice when conducted as part of a well-regulated, even-aged management system. Within that system partial cutting is essential as a tool for stand improvement and thinning; it must also be part of the over-all management plan.

Although clearcutting is seen as a sound silvicultural practice, it is a method which should not be practiced on steep slopes or on slopes with highly erodible soils. It is inappropriate in areas which get heavy recreational use. Where the dominant form of land use is intensive outdoor recreation, other methods—possibly only salvage cuttings—are indicated. In no case should the annual harvest average more than 1 or 2 percent of the area of the total management unit.

To ensure adequate allocation of land for both recreation and timber harvest, land should be zoned. Timber producing

77

Rhododendrons grow quickly where the western Oregon forest has been cut. For a few years the freshness of the deep green foliage and bright pink blossoms stands in sharp contrast to the jagged, blackened stumps, but soon the rhododendrons and small Douglas fir trees grow tall and the appearance of devastation is replaced by healthy young growth.
Photo, D. Burwell

sections should be planned specifically where timber production is an economically and socially desirable form of land use.

Intensive recreational demands are often concentrated on stream valley and lower slope sites. Unfortunately these are the same sites where timber production has the greatest potential because of better growth, species variety and low-cost accessibility. For this reason as well as for many others it is imperative that land planning be carried out and weighed carefully by groups representing a wide variety of fields of expertise.

4

Clearcutting of Public Forests in the Southern Pine Region

by
Charles W. Ralston
Dean and Professor of Forest Soils
School of Forestry
Duke University

THIS REPORT REVIEWS the evolution, rationale, status, and ecological implications of timber management practices on public forests in the southern pine region. Our major emphasis is on examination of the environmental consequences of the clearcut system of even-age management that has been the dominant harvesting method in this region for two decades, and which recently has become a topic of wide public interest and concern.

Some individuals who object to clearcutting question its compatibility with the sustained yield, multiple-use concept that is the basic principle for management of public forest lands. Other groups are disturbed by the esthetic appearance of clearcut areas and are able to show numerous examples that support their views. Claims also have been made that clearcutting has serious adverse effects on water quality and that timber harvesting by this method will ultimately lead to significant decrease in the productivity of forest sites.

Most of the information needed to prepare a rational evaluation of the role of clearcutting in southern pine silviculture and management has already been accumulated and is available for review, but effects of management practices on nutrient content of streamflow cannot be appraised until such studies are initiated and reported.

Our analysis refers mainly to national forest lands in the Piedmont, Coastal Plain, and Mississippi Delta provinces of the southeastern U.S. National forests and parks in the southern Appalachians are not included in our evaluation, nor are military reservations or other federal lands where timber production is not a primary activity. Thus, we are speaking of an aggregate of 5 million acres of public forests in 10 southern states, reaching along the Gulf Coast from Texas to Florida and north along the Atlantic Coast to Virginia. Most of these lands were cutover, burned-over woodlands or submarginal old fields at the time when they were established as national forest purchase units during the depression years of the 1930's.

Since that time they have been protected from wildfire and managed to produce stands of longleaf, slash, loblolly, and shortleaf pines, the principal species of value that will grow reasonably well on the sandy soils of the Coastal Plain or on the clay uplands of the Piedmont after two centuries of agricultural abuse. With exception of two small forests in the Mississippi Delta, productive hardwood sites are found only along bottomlands of streams that drain the Piedmont region and along the edges of poorly drained bays and swamps that guard the headwaters of coastal estuaries and marshlands of the Lower Coastal Plain.

It is important to realize that these forests exhibit for the most part typical features of the southern pinery, e.g., summer heat and humidity, snakes, ticks, deerflies, and chiggers. While there are some spots with great appeal to people who have become accustomed to such discomforts, the principal opportunity for developing high quality recreational experiences is in the mountain forests of the South.

THE EVOLUTION OF SILVICULTURAL SYSTEMS IN THE SOUTH

Those early Spanish explorers DeSoto and Ponce de Leon had a leisurely look and intimate contact with the forests from the Carolinas to Texas and remarked about the endless trees—not so much with admiration of the world's most extensive pine forest, but with fear of the cover for hostile Indians and dangerous animals. Even John Bartram several centuries later dismissed these forests as "dreary pine barrens."

As elsewhere, the early settlers of the South considered the forest as a barrier to agriculture and so cleared extensive areas to make room for more and more cotton fields. And although there were scattered sawmills cutting selected trees, particularly old-growth longleaf pine, the only forest product in commerce was naval stores.

Many of the cotton fields were abandoned following the War Between the States and these, including the areas cleared of oaks and hickories in the Piedmont, were quickly taken over by dense stands of loblolly and shortleaf pines.

By and large, however, at the beginning of this century the great original forests of the South were still intact. But about that time the lumber industry had thoroughly cut over the Lake States, moved rapidly into the South and within 30 years or so cut much of its forests. Indeed, in the peak year of 1909 the South produced nearly one-half of the nation's lumber—21 billion board feet. Vast areas were completely clearcut, particularly the extensive longleaf pine forests of the Gulf States, but there was generally somewhat more selective cutting in the South Atlantic States. This was strictly an economic selection cutting—or high-grading—removing only the biggest and the best, for there was no profit in small trees, and a preference for longleaf pine rather than the inferior loblolly.

By 1930 the old forest had been badly mauled and most of the larger lumber mills closed out or moved West. It was during the early and mid-thirties that the national forests in the southern pine and Piedmont regions were acquired and organized (the Ocala and Bankhead Forests were established somewhat earlier) to manage the remnants. It was also during this period that something remarkable happened. As the states began effective control of wildfires, a new forest developed—a "second-growth" forest—on much of the cutover land, augmented by the seeding-in of extensive areas of farm land abandoned during the late twenties and early Depression years. This was nature's reply to those who had resigned themselves to the inevitable doom of the South's great forest resource.

It was also about this time that the forest conservation movement made new advances: the acquisition of new national forest lands, the Civilian Conservation Corps, the Lumber Code of the National Recovery Act, and the persistent threats of federal regulation of forest practices on private timberlands. There seems to be no doubt that as a reaction to the great clearcuttings of the old growth forest, the U.S. Forest Service advocated "selective cutting" in all its forest types, and this became synonymous with "conservation." For the southern pine types, the most extensive being loblolly pine, this meant selective cutting in the remnant forest: too young, small, and unprofitable to cut earlier in the century. Many of these stands, now merchantable, were "partially cut," leaving about half the volume to be "stored on the stump."

This form of management met with scattered opposition, led by Professor H. H. Chapman who insisted that the imposition of any one silvicultural system to all forest types and conditions without regard to silvical characteristics was a terrible mistake. He further insisted that the classic "selection system" had been deliberately re-defined to come to mean the elimination of clearcutting as a silvicultural technique and even-age as a stand characteristic. In effect, the selection system was to be a panacea to avoid the threat of overcutting and "to solve at one stroke the dual problem of sustaining local supplies of timber and the renewal of the forest." Chapman believed that the Forest Service was trying to promote forest conservation by convincing landowners that frequent cuttings on the same area would reduce the time lag in securing income from the timber crop. Although he did not seriously question the principle where applicable, Chapman did indeed object to its application in the southern pines.

82

Support for Professor Chapman's objections grew as foresters in the South observed the effects of partial cuttings. It became apparent that such techniques plus the necessary exclusion of fire would lead to the invasion of hardwoods into the pine stands. On all but the most productive soils these hardwoods would be of low quality, would eventually occupy a significant portion of the site, and ultimately lead to reduced yields of quality timber.

But not all foresters agreed. There were those in the western part of the loblolly pine region—Alabama, Mississippi, and Arkansas—who were equally convinced of the merits of the selection system. They believed that higher-quality products could be grown under the all-aged system (and they were probably right) and that such management would be profitable; of this, there is sharp disagreement.

By 1950 the evidence grew so strong in favor of even-aged management of the southern pines along the Atlantic coastal region, that the management plan for the Francis Marion National Forest proposed the use of the seed-tree system for regeneration of the pine working group. This system was soon extended to the entire southern region of the U.S. Forest Service for both pines and hardwoods. And now, with the uncertainties of natural regeneration and the advances in tree improvement, the seed-tree system is being replaced by clearcutting with artificial regeneration.

The only thing in common with the current clearcutting system and the clearcutting during the early part of the century is the term itself. To many people that term implies over-cutting the forest, no concern with its renewal, and defiance of the principle of multiple use. Such misconceptions are difficult to correct and the task of restoring public confidence in management practices on federal lands is a major challenge to forest administrators.

HARVESTING NATIONAL FOREST TIMBER

Several concepts need to be briefly stated, perhaps over-simplified, so as to follow the procedures used in the management of the national forests and the harvesting of the timber crop.

Even-aged management presupposes growing each timber crop to a predetermined age—"Rotation Age"—and harvesting the crop at that age by clearcutting, seed-tree, or shelterwood systems. When a balanced distribution of age classes has been attained, an area equal to the number of acres in the working group, divided by "rotation," will be harvested and regenerated each year. This is referred to as "the annual regeneration objective."

Rotation ages are selected on the basis of rates of growth, resistance to disease and insects, financial and social considerations; these vary according to species and location. In the South, for example, the rotation age of the yellow pines ranges from 60 to 80 years, that of hardwoods from 80 to 100 years, with a 50-year rotation for such short-lived species as sand pine.

In fully stocked managed forests with equal distribution of age classes, the allowable annual cut of all products should equal the net growth that the site can produce. However, because of the past land-use practices in the South there is a preponderance of young stands and serious shortages in growing stock in the older stands. This imbalance, both in age-class distribution and in growing stock, requires that adjustments be made.

It is usual practice, and the national forests follow this procedure, to adjust both the "annual regeneration objective" and the "regulated allowable cut" so as to proceed toward the desired pattern of fully stocked stands and balanced age classes. This usually requires cutting fewer acres than normal and something less than the actual growth.

For the Southern National Forest Region as a whole in 1970, the annual regeneration objective was set at 169,114 acres applied to the unreserved available area of 10,910,400 acres—meaning that approximately a sixty-fourth of the area would be harvested that year through clearcutting, seed-tree, or removal cuttings. Actually 168,000 acres were cut—just about as planned.

As far as *quantity* of timber is concerned, during the past 10 years approximately 8.6 billion board feet of timber products were cut and sold. This was 17 percent less than the planned regulated allowable cut for the period. However, for those forests where the southern pines are the major forest types, the actual cut was essentially as planned (98 percent of the annual allowable cut).

It appears, then, that the national forests are holding fairly well to their planned harvest of timber. As to whether the plans reflect conservative practices and are in accordance with the previously stated objectives of building up growing stock, we must rely upon the following statement of the Regional Forester:

"... National Forest standing timber inventories over the same period (the past 10 years) have increased about 30 billion board feet of sawtimber to about 42 billion—a 40 percent *increase*. In addition, cordwood volumes have increased from 54 million cords to 82 million cords—a 52 percent increase. This build-up of standing timber inventories by the process of cutting less timber than is being grown will continue for many decades, or until optimum sustained yield capacity is reached.

Any implication, therefore, that the National Forests of the South are being over-cut has no basis in fact."

There is no evidence to the contrary.

REPRODUCING CUT-OVER AREAS

Foremost among the basic concepts of forestry is the goal of securing a continuous flow of products from a given forest indefinitely. This can be achieved only by ensuring that mature trees are systematically replaced by new trees.

No system of forest management, whether it be even-aged or all-aged, and no method of harvesting, whether it be clearcutting or selection, is acceptable unless there is assurance of the renewal of the forest. It would be myopic, then, to examine the management systems of the national forests without inquiring of the adequacy of the procedures for regenerating the cut-over areas.

Being committed to even-aged management, the national forests of the South rely largely upon artificial methods of forest renewal: planting and direct seeding. Natural methods are employed to some degree, such as the seed-tree system and the opportune use of available advanced reproduction by removal cuttings; and for many hardwoods, coppice regeneration.

The preference for planting and seeding in the pine types is quite apparent because of the greater certainty of restocking at acceptable levels, and because of the obvious benefits of improved genetic quality.

Analysis of available data shows that during the four-year period 1967-1970, some 270,000 acres of softwoods were clearcut; during the same period 236,985 acres—or 85 percent—were either planted or seeded. It is recognized that a time-lag, perhaps a year or two, frequently exists between the cutting operation and planting, so the discrepancy is not unexpected.

The national forests are aware that any method of forest regeneration, even planting, does not guarantee stand establishment. Provision is made for continuous inventory of regeneration, beginning with the third year. Remedial action is taken if acceptable stands are not present.

It is important to recognize that the southern pines are temporary types in an ecological succession that culminates in an oak-hickory climax forest throughout most of the region. The abundance of pine forests in the South are testimony to a long history of wildfires and abandoned fields that created countless clearings for their establishment. During the pine stage of succession—after the canopy closes—first, birds perch and distribute seeds of lesser trees and shrubs (as dogwood, redbud, and red cedar); later, as the forest habitat becomes more suitable for them, squirrels and other large rodents hide nuts of oaks and hickories at more places than they can remember, so these species become established in the understory. All of these trees can survive and grow under the shade of the pine overstory, whereas pine seedlings cannot. When natural mortality or cutting removes the pine overstory, the hardwood understory is released and dominates the site. Therefore, pine silviculture hinges on the control of understory vegetation during the rotation or on its removal at the time when the site is to be regenerated to pine. Frequently, prescribed burning at appropriate intervals will suffice for control of understory brush during the rotation period. More often, however, more drastic measures for site preparation are required after harvesting to control undesired vegetation or to remove impediments so that mechanized equipment can be used for planting. Sometimes, too, "bedding" is needed on the moist sites.

These treatments are costly—prohibitively so for selection systems—but if kept at a moderate level, the short-term returns seem to be quite favorable. But there may indeed be damaging long-term effects from the use of heavy equipment, particularly in the movement of debris. Indications are that the windrowing of logging slash and unmerchantable trees results in unavoidable moving of top-soil, which can seriously degrade productive quality of sandy soils and possibly that of deeper soils on moist sites as well. While these effects deserve more detailed study, it is urged that the national forests proceed with caution in using heavy equipment for site preparation that might cause compaction or lateral displacement of soils.

ECONOMIC SIGNIFICANCE OF WOOD PRODUCTS

According to Forest Service reports, the national forests of the South have supplied wood-using industries with over 5 billion board feet of sawtimber, and more than 6 million cords of pulpwood during the past 10 years, under the even-aged system of management and its associated methods of cutting, including clearcutting.

This production may have had local significance, but hardly a major impact on the forest products economy of the region, for it represents only about 5 percent of the lumber and about 2 percent of the pulpwood supply in the South.

Even so, the sale of timber products has an important effect upon local communities and political sub-divisions. The national forests in effect "pay taxes," since 25 percent of the gross receipts are returned to the counties. During 1970 the national forests in the South paid the states an average of about 40 cents per acre, mostly from the sale of timber. Any reduction in allowable cut would have serious consequences in the financing of local governments.

It should be noted, however, that national forest timber must make a much greater contribution to the regional timber supply during the next several decades if the projected future demands are to be met. Estimates are that the demand for sawtimber and plywood in the South will be almost double the current cut by the year 2000. Since it is presumed that the 22 million acres of timberlands owned by the pulp and paper companies will be operated for pulpwood production on short rotations, and since it is quite likely that a large percentage of the small private woodlot owners will continue to orient their timber toward the pulpwood market, the burden of producing an increasing supply of high-quality sawtimber and plywood will fall on the publicly-owned lands. It is simply uneconomical for private timberland owners to grow large-size, high-quality trees at prevailing and projected stumpage prices for such products. Furthermore, implementation of forestry practices that would increase the supply of pulpwood from vast acreages in small private woodlots throughout the South cannot be justified at current open market prices in most areas. Recent proposals for federal "incentive programs" to promote better forestry on

88

small woodlots are, in fact, subsidies that will maintain present low-cost raw material advantages of the wood industries and that will be paid by the unsuspecting taxpayer who will receive no benefit in the price of finished commodities.

COMPATIBILITY OF CLEARCUTTING
AND OTHER FOREST USES

Multiple use of public lands generally is regarded as a worthy management principle, but in practice it is a concept that causes difficulties because it has never been defined by the managing agencies in a way that has received general public acceptance. It is widely known that multiple use management is supposed to provide timber, water, wildlife, grazing, and recreation benefits from public lands. However, serious problems arise when either the using public expects certain special interest uses to be provided on every acre, or when managers emphasize timber production without proper regard for other use values. If the latter attitude prevails it should be apparent that indiscriminate application of the clearcut system of even-aged management produces the greatest impact on other forest uses. While effects of clearcutting on management for water, animals, and recreation can be significant, the matter of compatibility with other uses—or lack of it—is not an inherent property of the cutting system, but rather of how well the cutting plan is integrated with other use priorities.

EFFECTS OF WATER MANAGEMENT

Complete removal of forest cover causes changes in the quantity, quality, and seasonal distribution of water flow from forested watersheds.

Quantity of Water—Water yield increases after clearcutting because the forest canopy no longer intercepts rain and no longer transpires water supplied to tree crowns by roots deep

89

within the soil. If the soil is shallow (less than 18 inches), timber cutting has little effect on water yield, because evaporation will remove most of the water from shallow soils even where there is no vegetation. However, on soils where trees are deeply rooted, increase in water yield up to 16 inches per year has been measured after clearcutting. Such large increases in flow occur only in areas of high annual rainfall (more than 60 inches per year) on sites with deep permeable soils. For average conditions in the South, complete timber removal increases streamflow by about half this amount (eight inches per year).

Maximum difference in streamflow from clearcut and comparable forested watersheds occurs during the first year after cutting; then the difference in water yield diminishes progressively over a five- to 20-year period (depending on soil depth) as the new stand reoccupies the soil and crown space of the harvested stand. When considering the impact of clearcutting on water yield, it is quite important to recognize the general as well as the local consequences of this cutting practice. The overall effect can be visualized by assuming sustained yield management of a 100,000-acre forest on a 100-year rotation using the clearcut regeneration system. This implies that one-hundredth of the forest area (1000 acres) is clearcut and regenerated each year during the rotation. If the annual cutting is concentrated in one block, and if a flow increase of eight inches per acre is effected, there will be substantial increase in discharge of streams in the clearcut block (8000 acre-inches). If the annual cut is obtained from 10 cutting units of 100-acre size and is dispersed over the entire forest area, the impact on flow of individual streams is reduced considerably. If average annual rainfall is 40 inches, it is apparent—irrespective of the harvesting method—that the annual effect of cutting one-hundredth of the forest area, can cause only a 0.2 percent increase (in this case, 0.08-inch per acre) in water outflow from the entire forest area. However, if our evaluation is expanded to include cumulative increases in water yield over a 10-year cutting and forest re-establishment period, the average flow increase would be four inches per acre from 10,000 acres, or a 1 percent increase in runoff for the forest as a whole.

Annual harvests of similar volumes of timber by any other method, including the selection system, would generate similar increases in streamflow from the entire forest, but the amplitude of local fluctuations in streamflow would decrease if the annual cut is taken from smaller units, more widely dispersed over the forest area. Adoption of shorter harvesting rotations would effect proportionate increases in water yields, e.g., a 2 percent increase, if the subject property were managed on a pine sawtimber rotation of 50 years, or a 5 percent change in outflow, if a 20-year pulpwood rotation were implemented.

Water Quality—Alterations in quality of streamflow will occur whenever natural forest ecosystems are disturbed by any human use activity. When livestock, game, timber harvesting, or recreational usage becomes concentrated in the vicinity of streams, lakes, ponds, or reservoirs, the water receives varying amounts of erosional sediments, dissolved and suspended organic substances, and soil leachates containing several kinds of inorganic salts.

Consequently, if one's purpose is to maximize water purity, then all other use activities should be prohibited on watershed lanes. Since this option is seldom available on public forests, it seems sensible to insist that the water-supply administrator have authority to regulate other use activities in areas where high quality water is scarce. Otherwise, the recreation director, range specialist, or timber manager is apt to emphasize his interest at the expense of water quality.

The most serious threat to maintenance of water quality is from soil sediments that may enter streams during the construction or subsequent use of forest roads. Although this threat exists, it is important to understand that a forest without roads is an unmanaged wilderness, and that it cannot be used for any other purpose, or even be protected from wildfire, disease, and insect attack.

Serious siltation of streams from forest roads can be avoided by proper road location, by establishing roadbank vegetation, and by installing devices to divert road wash into areas where the water will be filtered through the soil before reaching stream channels.

The extent to which clearcutting or other harvesting methods contributes to sediment load of streams depends largely on the way that logging is done. If timber is cut to the stream bank, and if operators are given freedom to skid logs across or down stream channels, large volumes of sediment can be expected. When careless logging was permitted on test sites at the Coweeta Hydrologic Laboratory in the southern Appalachians, water turbidity on the logged area averaged 93 parts per million as opposed to 4 parts per million on an adjacent undisturbed watershed. Sediment loads reached a maximum of 7000 parts per million during a major storm on the logged area and 80 parts per million on the control watershed. Study of a commercially clearcut area on the Fernow Experimental Forest in the central Appalachians revealed average maximum turbidities of 490 parts per million during the cutting period and no detectable sediment in water from the undisturbed control watershed. In this same study, two watersheds, logged by extensive and intensive diameter limit selection methods and with logging regulations to prevent disturbance of stream margins, gave maximum turbidities of 210 and 25 parts per million, respectively. The Fernow study also indicated that damage to water quality decreased rapidly after logging disturbance ended. On the commercial clearcut site, average turbidity was 490 ppm during logging, 38 ppm one year after, and 1 ppm two years after logging. Rapid regrowth of protective vegetational cover was the principal factor causing quick recovery of water quality.

While we maintain that prevention of soil erosion from roads or logging is the most critical factor in protecting water quality of public lands, questions recently have arisen about increases in concentrations of dissolved inorganic ions, particularly nitrate,

Logging here at Union Pass in Teton National Forest has left unsightly residue and has stripped the cover from a small pond.　　Photo, U. S. Forest Service

Here on Lower Spread Creek, Teton National Forest, timber harvest has been planned and adjusted to protect a pond.　　Photo, U. S.Forest Service

found in streamflow after clearcutting. In reality, studies exploring such relationships have been few in number and it will be several years before the results of more definitive studies will be available for evaluation. The work that has received wide attention of environmentalists is that of investigators at Hubbard Brook Experimental Forest who found significant increases in concentrations of nitrate in streamflow following clearcutting. They observed that maximum nitrate levels exceeded standards set by the Public Health Service during certain periods after cutting and also inferred that clearcutting causes serious depletion of soil nitrogen and hence would lead to degradation of site productivity. The experimental treatment which produced these conclusions consisted of clear felling a beech-birch-maple forest leaving all material in place on the ground, and killing all vegetational regrowth on the area for three successive seasons by spraying with herbicides. With no vegetation to reabsorb nitrates released by microbial decomposition of plant remains and soil organic matter, and with increased leaching caused by absence of vegetation (transpiration was eliminated), nitrate concentration in stream water peaked at 18 ppm in the fall of the second year of treatment (1967) and was above 6.8 ppm in the spring and summer. Herbicide treatments were stopped in 1968, and in the fall of 1970, after two seasons of vegetational regrowth, nitrate levels of the clearcut watershed at Hubbard Brook had declined to 2.8 ppm, a value quite close to those measured at four other clearcut areas now being monitored in the White Mountains of New Hampshire. While data on effects of clearcutting on nitrate levels of stream water are as yet inadequate for authoritative judgments, evidence collected so far indicates that average levels are about 3 ppm in the peak period following clearcutting as opposed to 0.3 ppm in undisturbed forest areas. If effects of this magnitude are confirmed, there is little reason to worry about health hazards, and if long-term depletion of soil nitrogen is a matter of ecological concern, soil fertility can be restored or enhanced by judicious applications of nitrogen fertilizers. One

94

should remember also, as in the case for regulating quantity of streamflow, that the impact of clearcutting on release of nutrients into individual streams can be moderated a great deal by reducing the size and increasing the dispersion of annual cutting units.

Seasonal Distribution of Streamflow—In the South, maximum streamflow occurs during winter and early spring, a period when vegetation is dormant and soil water storage space is virtually saturated, and then diminishes during the growing season when current precipitation does not replace transpiration losses. After logging of southern pines, streamflow from clearcut areas can be expected to increase during the following summer by an amount equivalent to the reduction in transpiration loss.

A particular facet of the effect of timber cutting on water regimes that deserves attention is its influence on groundwater levels in loblolly pine types on fine-textured soils in the flatwoods of the Atlantic Coastal Plain. Observations of water levels in wells in a selection forest and a nearby stand prior to cutting indicated greater depths to groundwater in the more densely forested areas scheduled for clearcutting. After cutting, the water table in wells in the center of clearcut strips was 7½ feet higher following heavy rains during the growing season than levels recorded for wells in the selection forest. Drainable pore volume in these heavy clay soils is so small (around 10 percent) that changes in soil water as a result of eliminating transpiration are magnified by a factor of ten in producing water table effects.

EFFECTS ON FISH AND GAME MANAGEMENT

Interrelationships of timber cutting practices and the management of fish and wildlife have been studied in greater detail than any of the other multiple use aspects of southern forest management. The habits and requirements of major native and introduced game species are adequately known, and federal, state, and many private timber management agencies have professional wildlife specialists who attempt to maintain flourishing populations of these animals. More recently, public land administrators have recognized the importance of protecting rare or endangered species of plants and animals and now have operating programs to preserve these life forms for future enjoyment.

Controversies about cutting practices and their influence on wildlife populations usually are local matters that are brought to public notice by sportsman or nature groups who see that their interests are threatened by timber management practices. However, these conflicts are more apt to arise over treatment of industrial forest land than from practices on land held in public ownership. A company decision, for example, to convert large areas of moist oak stream and swamp margins to pine types has a major impact on prime wildlife habitat and such programs will be resented and bitterly opposed by local hunters. Type conversion in this instance represents the most severe kind of clearcut from the viewpoint of the wildlife manager, but one should not conclude that type conversion should be prohibited everywhere on public forests because there are many sites in the South that are incapable of growing good hardwoods, and these lands should be converted to pine.

The compatibility of clearcut silvicultural systems and management for wildlife purposes can become a matter of concern on public lands in the South only when timber management specialists violate established guidelines of wildlife specialists. Current directives requiring better quality and balance in multiple use programs are helpful in this regard.

Specific relationships between timber harvesting systems and game management deal primarily with the water, food and cover requirements of various animal species that have management potentials in local environments. In the southern pine region, the key habitat areas for most wild species are the hardwood bottoms and swamp margins, and if care is taken to protect these areas from indiscriminate cutting disturbance and

96

type conversion, a major share of success in maintaining abundant animal populations will be assured. This is not to say that managers should ignore opportunities to preserve critical habitat niches in upland areas, e.g., squirrel dens and nest trees of the red-cockaded woodpecker, but merely to emphasize the crucial significance of bottomland forests to the habitat requirements of many southern wildlife species. The proper management of lake and stream margins is also vital to the maintenance of water quality for fishing and other aquatic sports, as well as for other water uses, and these activities deserve much respect in planning timber harvesting systems for such areas.

If literature on relations between silvicultural harvesting methods for upland forests and their relative merits for wildlife is studied it will be found that game food is most abundant in clearcut openings. Complete removal of the forest canopy admits full sunlight and increases supplies of soil moisture and nutrients for use by lesser vegetation. Annual grasses and herbs rapidly invade cutover areas and perennial shrubs and tree sprouts grow and fruit more vigorously, thereby providing more food and cover patches for grazing, browsing, and seed-eating animals. However, if clearcut openings are too large, food supplies distant from the uncut forest edge are of little value to species that become easy prey when they stray too far from tree cover. Consequently, width of clearcut units in relation to the territorial habits of the animals featured for management is the most significant design characteristic in arriving at a harvesting plan that is suitable for both timber and wildlife production. The absolute size of cutting units is not highly critical and is determined less predictably by the distribution pattern of key habitat areas and the overall dispersion and diversity requirements for other use purposes.

Clearcutting does not have an appreciable effect on fish culture as long as stream bank vegetation is not removed. If stream margin stands are cut heavily, substantial responses to changes in microclimate may occur, particularly in small streams. An example of this effect was observed at the Coweeta Hydrologic Laboratory where the temperature of an open farm stream dropped from 80° to 68°F after passing through 400 feet of forested channel. The importance of stream margin vegetation to the maintenance of water quality, wildlife, and fish habitat justifies its identification as a protective zone where timber removal must be handled with great care.

EFFECTS ON GRAZING

Grazing of domestic livestock is not a very important use activity on southern public forest lands. Prior to World War II most of the beef cattle in the South were scrub stock that roamed about on unfenced wire grass ranges, maintained at marginal nutritional levels by annual burning. At this time, grazing permits on national forests were important to the local economy and production of range forage was a significant use function. After the war, southern soldiers, who had discovered that beef need not be tough, encouraged the growth of a new cattle industry based on high-value, registered stock raised on fenced, improved pastures and supplemental feeds. So now, although pasturage is still furnished on local demand and range specialists still claim some value for native forest range as a seasonal grazing supplement, it appears unlikely that range management will have a very significant role on public forests in the South.

Systems for integrating range, timber, and game plans, however, have been developed and demonstrated on forest ranges in Florida. The treatment consists of strip clearcutting of solid forest stands followed by fertilizing and seeding them with pasture grasses. The timbered zones are disked and planted with game food. Planned on a sustained yield basis, this operation will provide a steady flow of timber and beef and a suitable habitat to grow more deer, quail and turkeys. If the grassy strips undulate and are variable in width, the visual effect provides welcome relief to the rather monotonous slash and longleaf pine landscapes of the coastal flatwoods.

EFFECT ON RECREATION AND ESTHETICS

A large, square, clearcut block on the side of a mountain in distant view across a valley is an unpleasant sight to a motorist. It is upsetting to have direct evidence of man's disturbance of a lovely natural setting. If perceived at all, the facts that the area is being regenerated to new growth and that the wood harvest will satisfy many of his material needs do not erase his initial impression, nor his disapproval of people responsible for it. Foresters created this impression and they must answer to the public, revise their methods, and blend their cuttings into the natural landscape in a manner that is not distasteful to touring citizens. This kind of esthetic deterioration from clearcutting did not have to happen at all. In fact, if foresters simply take a good look at their natural surroundings, clearcutting can add beauty to the outdoor scene. Natural scars and openings as a result of fires, blowdown, landslides, insect attacks, and other causes are often abundant and they add visual diversity that relieves the monotony of long stretches of unbroken forest canopy. But these openings come in various sizes, shapes, and random patterns—never in large, square blocks—and though one often wonders what happened, there is nothing unnatural or uncomfortable about seeing them. Clearcut units, properly scaled in size and shape to accommodate near, intermediate, and distant viewing perspectives along main travel zones would add scenic value and remove this source of objection to timber cutting.

Another unpleasant aspect of clearcutting is the close-up view of a newly-cut area. Unless utilization is close and slash disposal is prompt and complete, the near view is enough of a shambles to convince the layman that the forest is being devastated.

However, such scenes are of short duration in the southern pine region if cutover areas are properly treated to insure prompt regeneration of the next crop of pine. Normally, after a sawtimber sale pulpwooders move in to clean up merchantable wood in tops and trees below sawlog size. Residual materials are

then cut into or close to the ground with drum choppers where they are less unsightly and will decompose more rapidly. Finally, the area may be burned and disked to expose a mineral soil bed for seeding or planting. Thus, the successful reestablishment of the southern pines depends on prompt and drastic reduction of logging debris, and provision of this silvicultural requirement greatly improves the appearance of clearcut areas. However, even when pine is not regenerated promptly, the viewer does not suffer very long, because pine silviculture hinges on holding back natural successional trends to hardwood types on all but the groundwater podzol soils of the longleaf-slash pine flatwoods. If the site is not prepared quickly, understory hardwoods are released by cutting, and in one or two seasons an effective screen of vegetation hides the logging residues.

Serious impact of clearcut management systems on other more specific recreational uses should not arise if special use areas are provided and respected, and if guidelines for the protection of water zones and key habitats for fish and game are followed. Perhaps the most useful data for judging effects of land management practices in producing environmental changes are obtained by monitoring water quality. A number of stations to measure such effects are now being planned throughout the national forest system in Region 8. If these plans receive high priority and early implementation, we will soon have facts instead of speculation to support the relative ecological merits of our management alternatives.

POLICIES AND PLANS TO ENHANCE PUBLIC BENEFITS FROM FEDERAL FORESTS

Perhaps the most encouraging result of this period of discontent with management practices on public lands is that it has stimulated the most thorough self-evaluation and reorientation of attitudes in the history of the Forest Service and other federal agencies with land management authority.

The main thrust of these reforms is summarized by a policy directive of the Chief of the Forest Service for all operational

Regeneration proceeds rapidly even on areas such as this one in Bighorn National Forest, which was subjected to a process in which logging residue was splintered by a roller-chopper some three years earlier. Photo, C. R. Batten

divisions "to do everything feasible to achieve better balance and improved quality in Forest Service management." Planning to implement this charge will be done at the regional level within the national guidelines.

STATUS OF PLANNING IN THE
SOUTHERN REGION

Since his appointment in 1968, the Regional Forester has given high priority to revamping concepts of forest resource management in Region 8 and to the development of planning systems and guides to direct field action programs. Main features of the new planning approach as given in *System for Managing the National Forests in the East* (1970) are:

1. Development of plans on a regional basis, e.g., in Region 8: Appalachian Mountains, Piedmont, Coastal Plain, and Ozark Highlands.
2. Organization and staffing of an interdisciplinary team to collect data needed to formulate overall regional guides and specific plans for the management of natural and human resources and protection of the environment within subordinate unit boundaries.
3. National forest boundaries exist only for administrative purposes in the development of *unit* plans. For management, the *unit* and its plan is determined by contributions of various portions of the national forest to the political, social, and economic well-being of the local region beyond its boundaries. This concept requires that *unit* boundaries be defined with the advice and counsel of state and local planning commissions and public officials.
4. The system provides for public input via hearings, tours, and written statements prior to development of the *unit* plan; public reviews after the draft plan has been prepared; and further public meetings whenever the *unit* plan is revised.

A guide for managing national forests in the Appalachians was issued in 1971. A new wildlife habitat handbook and visual

102

resource management guide also were distributed in 1971. These documents represent substantial efforts to reorient national forest systems to directions that should provide greater public benefit and enjoyment of federal forests in the South.

RECOMMENDATIONS FOR INTEGRATING TIMBER PRODUCTION WITH OTHER USES AND FOR MAINTAINING ENVIRONMENTAL QUALITY

While regional guides and unit plans propose new procedures for national forest management, most of the current criticism is about cutting practices, so public acceptance of the "new look" undoubtedly will depend on how well timber management practices blend with other uses and on their impact on environmental quality. Certain methods for reducing such impacts have been known for some time and merely need to be strictly observed at the operational level. Some of these things are designed for softening the effects of clearcutting, but there are other inherent difficulties with timber harvesting that must be dealt with—irrespective of the silvicultural system finally chosen—if perceptible damage to the environment is to be avoided. Several principles or procedures that deserve consideration in timber management planning are:

1. *Zoning*

   For at least seven years, management specialists in the southern region have recognized four zones that have value in planning timber harvesting activities. These are: *travel influence zones, water influence zones, special use zones,* and the *general forest zone,* which comprises the remainder and bulk of the area where timber production is viewed as a primary activity. Cuttings in travel zones must be planned to prevent undesirable aesthetic accidents and also to enhance viewing qualities. Water zones are vital to recreation, wildlife, and water quality and require most conservative harvesting treatments. Special use zones include recreation sites, wild and scenic areas, and places of unusual natural or human historical value that are to be preserved or developed with minimal disturbance.

2. *Clearcutting restrictions*

Current timber sale directives in Region 8 establish limits of 20-200 acres (ordinarily less than 100 acres) to size of clearcut areas. Furthermore, the shape and proximity of sale areas to other cutting blocks must be planned in accordance with guidelines prepared by landscape specialists. If district rangers have local problem areas in travel zones, cutting plans are to have advice of the landscape architect and approval of appropriate line officers.

Some lag time is being experienced in immediate application of these regulations, because some sale contracts written prior to their existence must be honored.

3. *Management type emphasis*

Current directives place much greater emphasis on management of hardwoods. All sites capable of growing good quality broad-leaved species are to be maintained or converted to these types. This policy recognizes and should perpetuate key habitats for wildlife and water protection zones.

4. *Forest roads*

Design, construction, use, and maintenance of forest roads is the most serious probable source of environmental difficulties and other use conflicts. The problem is perennial and will continue to be troublesome until a properly financed and regulated road program is developed.

Current regulations state that cost of road construction on National Forests is to be met from appropriations by Congress supplemented by money amounting to 10 percent of timber sale receipts reserved for road building, or indirectly by downward adjustment of stumpage prices, if the logger installs the road. This operational procedure contributes pressures that often lead to timber harvesting practices that are harmful to other use activities. The economics of road construction favors maximum timber removal and large cutting blocks to reduce unit road costs. Also, road locations are apt to follow routes that give easier and most direct access to timber sale areas at the expense of regard for other values. Thus, if the public land manager attempts to optimize timber harvesting economics, he is forced into a path that may lead to severe public criticism.

The road problem is national in scope and should have highest priority for study and solution. The Forest Service maintains that operator-built roads cause most of the harmful effects and that funds should be provided so that all roads could be designed and maintained by Forest Service engineers. Establishment of a revolving fund to be repaid from timber sale receipts has been suggested as a possible solution to this problem. In any event, the road problem is a key question in the environmental management of our public forests.

5. *Harvesting equipment*

A major trend in the development of harvesting equipment for the Southeast and elsewhere may bring about significant long-term decrease in soil productivity. This trend was triggered by increased labor costs that forced the forest industries into doing their own harvesting by highly mechanized methods. Since the cutting units are usually large (about 1000 acres) and the pulp mill must be fed 24 hours a day, efficiency called for larger and larger machines that could plow through cutting areas in any kind of weather. It has been shown that soil compaction, puddling, and disruption of surface drainage during logging has detrimental effects on subsequent establishment and growth of loblolly pine on fine-textured soils of the Lower Coastal Plain. While it is assumed that tillage in site preparation will correct the damage, this assumption has not yet been established.

The main point here, however, is that Forest Service sale areas tend to be logged in the same way and with the same equipment that is used elsewhere in the region. Possibly this should not be the case, and perhaps the Forest Service could provide leadership in the development of smaller machines with decreased bearing pressures to minimize soil disturbance in logging. Current directives for decrease in size of cutting areas, emphasis on hardwood management, and environmental protection indicate that specifications for the design of harvesting equipment deserve serious consideration.

6. *Research needs*

Forestry research in the southern region characteristically has been pragmatic and addressed to short range problems related to the silviculture, management, and utilization of pine. The current climate of public opinion has caused re-evaluation of research goals and projects are being renamed and reoriented to have some sort of ecological appeal. Although it would seem obvious that studies of environmental effects and multiple use management should have high priority, a few specific examples may illustrate the kinds of things that should be done:

a. External effects should be monitored for all studies of intensive silvicultural practices, e.g., forest fertilization, tillage, drainage, and prescribed burning. Similar data for even-age and all-age cutting systems also should be collected.

b. More attention should be given to hardwood research, particularly to artificial regeneration techniques.

c. More thought on social and economic aspects of forest amenity values is needed, and especially on how to shift costs of outdoor recreation from the general taxpayer to people who actually enjoy the benefits.

5

by
Robert E. Dils
Dean,
College of Forestry
and Natural Resources
Colorado State University

Clearcutting in the Forests of the Rocky Mountains

THE PRACTICE OF CLEARCUTTING in the Rockies has a relatively long and often colorful history. From the earliest times, clearcutting was an integral part of the pioneer days of western development. The expanding railroad system required large quantities of wood, primarily lodgepole pine, for ties. Consequently even-aged lodgepole stands of appropriate size were usually clearcut. To accommodate a booming mining industry, large areas of forest were cut to make mine props and to provide wood for local construction. With ranches and farms came the need for fenceposts, corrals and cabin poles. Later wood was needed for urban development including poles for telephone and power lines. More recently there has been a demand for wood for the large pulp mills in the Southwest and northern parts of the region, and pulpwood has been sent from the Rocky Mountain area to the pulp mills of the Lake States. Today there is an increasing demand for wood for plywood manufacture, for pallets, matchsticks and for packing material.

At first little thought was given by loggers to tree regeneration or forest management; to cleanup or to slash removal. Timber was there to be used for the growth and development of the region. After the early 1900's, however, a custodial ethic developed which led to research on forestry techniques in different areas and on different vegetational types.

As the tree associations of the area react differently to clearcutting six major commercial types have been identified and used as foci for this discussion. They are:

1. Ponderosa Pine
2. Lodgepole Pine
3. Spruce—Fir
4. Southern Mixed Conifers
5. Northern Mixed Conifers
6. Aspen

Present thought and forest management research virtually eliminate clearcutting of ponderosa pine. In most of the region today there is only limited clearcutting of this species.

Lodgepole pine, however, must be clearcut if the species is to be perpetuated. Experience has indicated that this type is maintained in nature only as a result of fire, insect, disease or other catastrophe. Nearly all the current lodgepole harvest is carried out by clearcutting.

The spruce-fir type is ecologically tolerant and can be grown under a variety of silvicultural systems to give either an even-aged or all-aged forest. It is shallow-rooted, however, so there is danger of considerable windthrow if harvest is carried out using either the seed tree or shelterwood techniques; thus it has become standard practice to clearcut. Clearcutting creates a problem for these species, however, as they are shade-tolerant and require cover for regeneration. To provide such cover a large amount of logging slash is left on spruce-fir areas. The debris, although unsightly, is silviculturally necessary.

Southwestern mixed conifers consist of a mixture of Douglas fir, white fir and ponderosa pine. Clearcutting has been used to harvest old growth and overmature stands but the recommended prescription for most of this type in the Southwest today is cutting by the shelterwood system.

In the northern parts of the region there is a variety of forest types which have been lumped together as northern mixed conifers. This group includes species with extremely diverse tolerances. Western larch is an intolerant species; western white pine and Douglas fir are moderately tolerant, while grand fir, subalpine fir, western cedar and western hemlock are distinctly tolerant. Within this mixture all forms of cutting have been prescribed but clearcutting has dominated, as the predominant objective of management has been timber production.

In some areas aspen is used commercially. In addition to commercial importance, it has unusual value for wildlife browse and in scenery management. Typically this species comes in rapidly on old burns and cutover areas as it regenerates from old roots and suckers. Where aspen is harvested it is usually clearcut.

Throughout the region and almost irrespective of forest types clearcutting has been applied as a sanitation technique as most of the forest types have been subject to outbreaks of fire, insect and disease epidemics. Bark beetles have caused damage over large areas of spruce while dwarf mistletoe affects large areas of lodgepole pine and of northern mixed conifers. In these cases, clearcutting has been used for sanitation purposes.

The patterns of clearcutting have changed considerably over the years. For reasons of convenience and supposed economy, clearcut areas were often quite large commonly exceeding 100 acres in size. More recently clearcuts have been smaller and have been made in patches or strips. Slowly they are being planned to provide more edge for wildlife, to provide esthetically desirable openings and to allow greater snow accumulations without impairing the watershed protection qualities of the forest. Such planning could be commonplace for the forester's "know-how" in applying clearcutting today is substantially greater than its applications indicate. The reasons for the disparity between theory and practice are related to matters of economics and policy rather than to any biological or physical limitations.

PRESENT STATUS

At the present time, approximately one-fifth of the commercial forest lands of the United States are in our national forests. Half of the total softwood inventory and 30 percent of the total harvest of softwood sawtimber comes from these forests. During 1970, a little over one-third of the timber land harvest acreage was clearcut. Significantly this third provided 60 percent of the total volume harvested. An examination of timber harvest in the national forests of the Rocky Mountain region is best carried out region by region as the area includes Forest Service Regions 1-4. (See map p. 111.)

During 1970, 50,000 acres or 57 percent of the total cut in Region 1 was clearcut while only 10 percent was treated by the shelterwood method. This clearcutting figure includes only acres which were clearcut in the conventional sense. Overstory removal, considered a form of clearcutting by some foresters, is included with the figures listed as "partial cut." If overstory removal were considered a form of clearcutting, which it may be in its visual impact, then this and all other "clearcut" figures would have to be somewhat higher to include acres harvested in this way.

For Region 2, partial cutting exceeded clearcutting over the five year period of 1966-70. If, however, one examines the figures for Region 2 and excludes logging done in the Black Hills and the San Juan National Forest, then almost all the cutting has been clearcutting.

About 75 percent of the forests in Region 3 are primarily ponderosa pine. These forests will be treated by methods other than clearcutting. Projections for timber harvest in this region are "almost negligible" whether considered in terms of volume or in terms of acres cut.

In Region 4, 60 percent of the area harvested was cut by the clearcut method during 1966-70. As for all the regions, detailed figures are available but they must be read with care as, in all cases, overstory removal is included as a partial cut method regardless of the intensity of the removal.

U.S. DEPARTMENT OF AGRICULTURE
FOREST SERVICE
EDWARD P. CLIFF, CHIEF

**NATIONAL FORESTS
AND FOREST SERVICE
FIELD OFFICES**

MILES
0   50   100   150   200

- NATIONAL FORESTS
- PURCHASE UNITS
- NATIONAL GRASSLANDS
- LAND UTILIZATION PROJECTS
- REGIONAL BOUNDARIES
- ⊙ REGIONAL HEADQUARTERS
- • SUPERVISOR'S HEADQUARTERS
- ▲ FOREST AND RANGE
  EXPERIMENT STATIONS
- ✳ LABORATORY (MADISON, WIS.)
- ☐ AREA DIRECTOR STATE AND
  PRIVATE FORESTRY PROGRAMS
- INSTITUTE OF NORTHERN
  FORESTRY
- ○ INSTITUTE OF TROPICAL
  FORESTRY

Clearcutting can be an extremely valuable tool for timber harvest, land management and silviculture. As a silvicultural system it is ecologically sound for certain forest types and sites. The problem is one of identifying and eliminating sites and species which are not suited to this form of harvest.

Where clearcuts have been performed on very steep and sensitive slopes the results have on occasion proved disastrous. Soil movement and erosion have resulted; regeneration has failed. In such areas even terracing efforts, designed to stimulate artificial regeneration, have failed. Such cuts and futile restoration efforts are both costly and esthetically displeasing.

Steep slopes are not the only areas which should be avoided. Dry soils are highly erodible and they too tend to deteriorate after a clearcut.

Concern has often been expressed regarding poorly executed clearcuts and their effects on soil erosion, sediment movement and water quality. Such effects may be due to poor logging practice but more commonly they are associated with poor road location, construction and maintenance.

To date there has been much concern with the unesthetic nature of clearcutting, specifically with the lack of cleanup after the logging operation. However, this apparent neglect is often a deliberate policy implemented for silvicultural reasons as it is in the spruce-fir forest. Clearcutting in large blocks produces even-aged stands which are sometimes overstocked. Such stands are not particularly pleasing from an esthetic standpoint. In addition to the esthetic objections to large clearcuts the crowded stands which grow and replace them make walking difficult and are not particularly productive of wildlife. If a stand of thick growth at poletimber stage covers an area of more than 100 acres it actually has negative habitat value.

Despite occasional errors and failures, clearcutting continues and the accusation has been levelled that the Forest Service, which allows such harvest, is over-concerned with timber production. Forest Service policy is an expressed response to the expressed goal of bolstering local economies, to the need for more forest products and better housing and to the wishes of Congress for more income in federal and local treasuries. Thus what appears as "failure" is actually a response to desires which, until five years ago, appeared to be the national goals. Those goals have changed and agencies are beginning to respond; perhaps they must do so more quickly.

IMPACT OF CLEARCUTTING

Some of the impacts of this practice are positive; others are negative. To appreciate the issues and to make the choices which must be made, an awareness of some of these impacts, influences and interrelationships is essential.

Site—The impact of clearcutting on the logging site depends on a variety of factors. It depends on the size and location of the area, the manner in which the clearcut was conducted, on post-cut treatment and on the initial site quality. Any influences will, of course, be most intense on poor sites; those with thin, rocky soil, south facing slopes, fragile subalpine areas, steep erosive slopes and very dry sites. The impact increases with increasing size of the area cut and with the amount of soil disturbance caused by road building, skid trails and landings. In addition the final condition of the site will be influenced by any post-logging treatment applied such as pile burning or broadcast burning of slash.

Climate—Within the clearcut area the microclimate changes after logging. Temperature extremes are amplified. It is warmer during the day and during the summer while it is cooler during the night and during the winter than it was previously. This cooling may present a problem as frost pockets may form which can inhibit regrowth of trees in the area.

Temperature—Diurnal and annual temperature cycles are intensified, as noted in the section on climate but this is not the only change which temperature alteration causes in the cutover area.

113

The increased day and summer temperatures cause an increase in biological activity which in turn leads to an increase in rate of decomposition of organic materials and, temporarily, in a more rapid release of nutrients to the soil. This effect is most pronounced on large cuts as a great area is exposed to increased sunlight. On small areas, however, the increase in solar radiation is coupled with restricted air movement so that again temperature rises. In addition, the changed reflectivity of the soil darkened by slash burning may intensify soil warmth. If sufficient heat is generated it may slow or even halt natural regeneration.

In the long run, however, the effects of clearcutting on site, climate and temperature are usually not significant. At times the successional pattern may be changed, mixed conifers may come back in different combinations from those cut, some sites are taken over by grasses, and occasionally the lower interface between spruce and lodgepole pine becomes blurred as the lodgepole invades spruce area. None of these changes alter the area materially.

Watershed—Forest lands and especially those of the national forests in the Rocky Mountain region show a distinct relationship to water yields and water quality. As much of the public forest land is in the high country where precipitation is high, any logging activity will affect water quantity, quality and timing. Research indicates that streamflow increase is roughly proportional to the decrease in forest cover, especially where soils are shallow. This was observed to be significant in a study performed at Fraser, Colorado in which it was also noted that despite the increased volume of flow, water quality remained high. If, however, there is significant soil disturbance during logging and if the cut is on steeply sloping land, there may be serious erosion resulting in siltation problems and an accompanying degradation of water quality. Such heavy sedimentation would be harmful to trout as it could destroy spawning beds. In some cases, however, mountain streams are so pure that

114

a modest amount of erosion might in fact add nutrients to the water and improve productivity from a fisheries standpoint.

Fishing interests have also been concerned with the rise in stream temperature which may accompany clearcutting. This may pose a problem but in many mountain streams at the higher elevations a little warming would be likely to lead to an increase in productivity rather than to a decrease.

Real damage to a watershed may occur as a result of a pile-up of debris in a stream. Such an accumulation can serve as a dam and may divert flowing waters. This would in turn cause channel erosion and an accompanying degradation of water quality. In fact, roads cause more damage than clearcutting so where watershed values are high and where harvesting operations are scheduled, the utmost caution should be observed in the location, construction and maintenance of the road system.

Wildlife—A basic statement of the interrelationship between wildlife and forestry was enunciated by Dr. Olof Wallmö (USFS Colo.) who observed the ecological principle that, "practices which diversify habitat generally provide more niches for more species and increase the carrying capacity for many species. Opening a forest canopy permits the development of ground level vegetation for use by ground-dwelling animals."

There is ample evidence that clearcuts of moderate size are beneficial to big game. Within the ponderosa and mixed conifers of the south, openings of up to 20 acres are beneficial to deer and elk. In lodgepole and spruce areas, however, it has been suggested that block clearcuts of 30 or more acres cause a decrease in deer and elk in the area. The decline in animal use of a clearcut is especially pronounced when there has been little or no slash cleanup. Dead trees, windfalls and slash all combine to make access to the cut area difficult. Good cleanup practices would enhance clearcut areas for wildlife use.

To date, the effect of clearcutting on animals other than deer and elk has been poorly documented. The practice may be detrimental to some species such as Alberts squirrels, which are

115

116

Understory vegetation is lacking in this overmature stand of lodgepole pine in Bighorn National Forest. There is no browse here. Fallen timber on the ground impedes movement of large animals and makes the area less than ideal for their use.

Photo, C. R. Batten

Two bull moose enjoy feeding on this clearcut area in Teton National Forest, Wyoming.

associated with mature ponderosa pine areas, or red-squirrels in the spruce-fir region. More such thinking as that reflected in Table A is needed. More attention must be directed to the type and pattern of cutting that will provide escape cover for big game; protection to calving grounds; runways, lakes, ponds and springs used by big game; habitat improvement and protection for birds and mammals and for human enjoyment of this resource.

Rangeland—In clearcut areas a variety of forage conditions develop which can provide grazing opportunity. After removal of the forest crop grasses, herbs and shrubs usually invade an area. Where regeneration is slow there is increased opportunity for lower vegetation to grow. This, in turn, retards tree re-establishment favoring still more growth of ground vegetation. If plantings fail and natural regeneration does not take place on spruce-fir areas, full conversion to grass or rangeland may be expected.

In the past, areas turned to grassland by logging have been used as pasturage for domestic cattle and sheep. As clearcuts become smaller and further apart this will become more difficult and use will dwindle until the grassy patches are used only by browsing wildlife.

Recreation—This is the area in which the impact of clearcutting is greatest and where the opponents of the practice are most vocal. Opinions vary depending on the type of recreation sought. Unquestionably clearcutting is unacceptable to those who require the primitive environment for their pleasure. At the other end of the spectrum clearcutting is essential in the development of ski trails. Other forms of recreation may benefit by clearcuts which are well placed and timed. A clearcut which increases streamflow may well improve fishing in a given stream. Clearcut openings and overlooks can improve horseback trails. They can create spaces and views for cross country skiing and snowmobiling. They can even open up scenic overlooks and

Table A. Approximation of effects of clearcutting on wildlife on
Kaibab Plateau, Arizona, Region 3 U.S. Forest Service

+ = Beneficial Effect   - = Detrimental Effect

Species	Spruce-fir	Species	Spruce-fir
Deer	+	Cougar	+
Coyote	+	Weasel	+
Bobcat	+	Porcupine	-
Ground squirrel	+	Chipmunk	+
Red squirrel	-	Pocket gopher	+
Meadow mouse	+	Sharpshinned hawk	+
Western red tailed hawk	+	Desert sparrow hawk	+
Dusky grouse	+	Red shafted flicker	+
Williamson's sapsucker	-	White breasted woodpecker	-
Alpine three-toed woodpecker	-	Wright fly catcher	-
Olive sided flycatcher	-	Violet green swallow	+
Mountain chickadee	-	Long crested jay	-
Audubon hermit thrush	-	American robin	+
		Mountain bluebird	+
Western ruby crowned kinglet	-	Audubon warbler	-
Evening grosbeak	-	Cassins purple finch	+
Pine siskin	-	Red backed junco	+
Western chipping sparrow	+		

119

enhance water scenes and rockscapes for the enjoyment of hikers and motorists.

Continuous even-aged forests, such as those of lodgepole pine, have a certain monotony of appearance. Well-designed and located clearcuts could add additional color and textural dimension to the landscape and would improve the esthetic qualities of the area. In addition such cuts might increase water yield and improve wildlife habitat.

Safety and Sanitation—Clearcutting has been used for safety purposes at road intersections as well as to open up sites in and around dwellings. It has been used to arrest the spread of insects such as bark beetles and diseases such as dwarf mistletoe. Occasionally it has been used along with some form of slash removal to reduce the fire hazard in particularly dangerous situations. Such specialized application will undoubtedly be continued and expanded as management becomes more intensive.

ALTERNATIVES

Selective logging can be utilized to a greater degree than is presently employed in certain forest types such as spruce-fir and mixed conifers. *Single tree selection* seems most advisable adjacent to campsites, between ski trails, along heavily travelled roads and highways, around lakes, ponds and scenic rocky outcrops. The *shelterwood* system is already heavily used in areas of ponderosa pine. It could also be useful in spruce-fir areas and in a variety of mixed conifer areas as long as the expected windthrow damage is anticipated to be low. This system of harvest might even prove useful in selected old stands of lodgepole pine. *Seed tree cutting* probably has less potential application in the Rocky Mountain region than any of the other systems available. The cost of the removal of the seed trees would be prohibitive and the danger of loss from windthrow would make the operation risky indeed; nevertheless experimentation with this method would be worthwhile. Seed tree cutting has potential applications in such types as lodgepole pine with non-serotinous cones and in certain mixed conifer types.

It is likely that more intensive and careful clearcutting in strips or patches offers the greatest opportunity in most of the Rocky Mountain forest types. Patches will undoubtedly be smaller than present clearcuts, five to 20 or 30 acres. Larger areas will be selected only where multiple use considerations, topography or economics dictate. Coordinated multiple use plans, including inputs from many specialties, should be a prime factor in determining the size and design as well as the location of these cuts. Salvage and sanitation cuts would undoubtedly continue as clearcuts although they too might be less extensive than they have been in the past.

SUMMARY

Multiple use activities and resources provided by the national forests can be optimized by carefully designed and executed forest cuttings including clearcutting. Well-planned cutting may improve water yield, enhance wildlife habitat, provide more pleasing and variable forest landscapes, improve browsing and grazing conditions and create new recreational opportunities. To make such improvements any timber harvest, whether clearcut or other, must be designed to fit into a wisely designed management plan.

There is a real lack of verifiable information on harvest methods and conflicting views are held by knowledgeable forestry professionals. Because of this there is increased public pressure on forestry officials who are unable to defend their management decisions. Much research is still needed. Among the areas which require further study are: insects and disease, natural regeneration windthrow, wildlife habitat, nutrient cycling, timber harvesting techniques, utilization standards, economics of alternative harvest systems, alternatives for meeting national wood needs, and impact on local economies.

121

122   The "Basketweave" cutting pattern shown here conflicts with the dominantly
horizontal landscape; the cuts appear awkward and unnatural.

123

Natural snow slide openings combine with well-dispersed man-made openings in Bridger National Forest to maintain an almost natural appearance despite clear-cuts.

Many significant issues surfaced during the course of this study; issues which should be given serious consideration when implementing current policies, revising them or formulating new ones. These issues are given no ranking or priority but should all be considered as all affect clearcutting practices and the quality of management of the public forests.

1. Multiple use management must be a working tool and must be accorded more than lip-service.
2. There is need for a more detailed system of forest zoning.
3. Some re-ordering of Forest Service priorities has become necessary.
4. Timber sales contracts need to be reviewed as, under present conditions, contracts cannot be renegotiated or altered to admit environmental improvements.
5. Attention should be paid to harvesting equipment and methods, especially those used on sensitive areas. Such considerations must be written into the sale contract.
6. There is need for a better way to assess road costs than by placing the entire cost burden on a single cut. This might be done by paying for the road through several cuts and by assessment for other uses.
7. There is need for improvement in timber sale administration and supervision.
8. A major effort is needed to effect more complete utilization of the forest crop, to increase efficiency and to prevent cleanup problems.
9. It is apparent that there has been an inadequate job of public relations, especially in educating the public as to why cuttings are made.
10. It is of the greatest importance to involve the entire profession and the public in the development of goals and priorities in public land management.
11. Some laws and concepts under which public agencies must act seem to be in conflict. Congress or the courts

will have to settle these conflicts to permit an orderly development of policy.

12. We need to think in terms of acre-by-acre management for we can no longer afford to operate by "prescription generalization" of forest types.

13. New guidelines should be developed with specific stipulations regarding types of areas which should not be clearcut.

14. More effort should be directed toward identification of high production timber sites and to the potential for yield improvement on those sites.

15. More opportunities are needed for new, imaginative techniques in forest land management.

16. There is need for a training program for foresters who will be putting multiple use plans together.

17. A major effort is indicated to try to make earlier determinations of what the public wants from its forests. As a start we should examine our failures to assess what is unpopular and why.

18. There is a credibility gap between part of the public and land management agencies. To regain public confidence the agencies should take every opportunity to consult with their associates on solutions to mutual problems.

6 | Clearcutting in the Pacific Northwest and Alaska

by
James S. Bethel
Dean,
College of Forest Resources
University of Washington

CLEARCUTTING IS A LONG ESTABLISHED form of forest removal. In the earliest days of a nation it is often used to clear lands for farms, roads and railways; for cities and for reservoirs. The major purpose of such cutting is simply to get the forest out of the way. But, clearcutting can also become a practice used to move a crop to market efficiently and inexpensively. Under this system, cutting is often conducted purely for short-term gain with little or no thought for the future of the land. Such was the forest-harvest system practiced in the early days of forest use in the U.S., a practice which came to be known as "cut out and get out."

Timber harvest has changed since those days, but the conversion from cutting for immediate gain to cutting as a considered forestry practice has occurred so gradually and recently that the distinction between the old and new types of logging is still not clear to many people.

Furthermore, the responsibility for any given harvest situation is unclear to most citizens. Indeed, the majority of people have no idea who owns any particular tract of land. This is especially true in the West, for here old patterns of land distribution have created a veritable checkerboard pattern of interspersed federal, state and private holdings. Thus, issues raised concerning the propriety of harvest practices are by no means necessarily directed at federal holdings.

126

In considering the federal lands it is important to remember that they are the property of all U.S. citizens; those who enjoy them as a source of beauty and recreation as well as those whose principal needs are for adequate low-cost housing, good schools, and moderate taxes. Increasingly, a growing segment of the American population has leisure time to pursue private interests among which outdoor activities rate high. As this is an exceedingly mobile group, people find easy access to many forests and forests are coming to be perceived as a source of amenities rather than as a source of employment and materials. The result has been increased conflict over whether the forests are primarily to be used for recreation or for timber.

Many forest users do not understand how national forest policy develops. Policy emerges from the political arena, a result of the complex interaction of pressure groups each with a specific interest. Decisions, therefore, are often based on attempts to compromise conflicting pressures rather than on scientific principle. The public forester must operate with a set of goals that is vague and changes rapidly. His task is to select, from the options open to him, courses of action which will achieve public goals while conforming, where possible, to the dictates of sound forestry practice.

But the goals confronting the manager are unclear with the result that land-use conflicts have arisen. Traditionally, the public forester has turned to rural communities and industry for goals, for these are the traditional power bases for determining forest policy. Today, foresters are still responsive to the needs of these groups. With the growth of environmental concern, however, urban populations have become concerned and new pressure groups have formed. These groups are sufficiently powerful that they are in a position to overwhelm the traditional power base.

The balance shifts quickly, but there is an inherent problem which slows the foresters' response. Forest-management decisions are necessarily long-term decisions, so foresters have come to think in terms of times which seem long to the layman but are short in relation to the life span of a tree. Public attitudes and policies, on the other hand, change on much shorter time cycles and harvest methods selected 20 years ago were based on different premises and a far different climate of public attitude than those which prevail today.

The focus on clearcutting as a modern problem stems from the rising concern with man's treatment of his environment. The visibility of the clearcut and its barely tolerable ugliness make it a ready symbol of rape. Again this is especially true in the West where, because of the checkered land-ownership pattern, cuts tend to have straight-line edges, management between areas is uncoordinated and the poor practices of any one owner reflect on all—for the average passerby cannot know the ownership of any particular sub-segment.

The issue of clearcutting is further compounded by the issue of utilization. Material left behind after a clearcut is regarded as waste by many—waste which, if used, might somehow reduce the need for cutting elsewhere. Waste is a problem, but it must be remembered that the material left in the woods is not usable under the present state of the art. In the forest, however, this material contributes to soil formation and to the nutrition of the succeeding crop of trees.

In part the problem is one of communication. During the mid-1960's, the Forest Service switched to clearcutting from other practices in certain regions. The reasons, merits and consequences of such a change, however, were never adequately explained to the public. The public saw only the appearance of the cutover landscape and reacted strongly to the fact that this seemed to be in direct conflict with the "wise" management which had been practiced earlier.

Of course there were and are occasions when clearcutting has been misapplied. For some high mountain species, on dry slopes, or where undesirable plants may usurp the site, it can be disastrous. Mistakes of this sort are invariably long lasting and painfully visible. However the history of natural catastrophe

128

within a forest—fire, landslides, floods, etc.—proves the tenacity of forests and the ability of injured forests to recover.

PRESENT STATUS

The forests of the Pacific Northwest are often considered to be the most magnificent natural coniferous forests in the world. Most of the original forest has been maintained in a subclimax state by the frequent occurrence of natural catastrophic disturbances. Those stands which consist of climax species frequently originated in mild disturbances so that they too have the even-aged structure usually associated with subclimax forests rather than the uneven-aged structure typical of climax stands.

Since the 1890's, the forests at lower elevations have been logged extensively. Where harvesting took place, areas are now occupied by young stands. To date, cutting has been carried out in a manner that, intentionally or not, has been an approximation of clearcutting and has had variable results. Most of the cut area has reforested naturally and in a very satisfactory manner. However, it has been estimated that 20 percent of the area occupied by young stands is considered to be unsatisfactorily stocked.

These even-aged stands, whether well stocked or not, continue to grow and in time a moment arrives when one generation of trees reaches the culmination of its value and should be replaced by another. Sometimes the natural processes of death and regeneration are appropriate, but these frequently lead to a forest species composition which is considerably less than optimal. Clearcutting is one of several methods used to remove the old stand and to replace it with a new one.

Clearcutting is used where it is desirable to reforest an area with trees of a species which grows best under conditions of exposure to full sunlight. This develops an even-aged stand which grows rapidly and is easy to operate and administer. And clearcutting is more than just a method for harvesting a mature

129

Natural wildfire caused a partial cut on this Oregon slope. After the fire, Douglas fir and hemlock seeded in, but the Douglas fir seedlings were unable to survive the shade. The hemlocks survived and grew but did not thin themselves out. These trees are over 110 years old but few are even one foot in diameter. The few large Douglas fir in the area are old and decadent. In time they will die and be replaced by the spindly hemlock unless the area is opened to sunlight.

Photo, D. Burwell

stand; it may be used, for example to convert a tract of undesirable vegetation to forest. Clearcutting may be used on tracts logged or burned long ago and since regrown to brush or a species of less than optimum value. On such areas it serves to salvage what useful material exists and to destroy the rest so that the site may be prepared for regeneration of desirable tree species. It is an appropriate method and sometimes the only method for salvaging timber after fires and for controlling insect and disease epidemics.

There are, of course, other methods by which trees may be harvested. The *seed tree* method is essentially similar to clearcutting except that a few trees are left on the area to provide a source of seed. The *shelterwood* method removes only a part of the old stand leaving a uniform partial stand. Once the critical first years of reproduction are complete and the overstory becomes a hindrance, the remaining trees are removed.

The *selection* method differs from the others in that it is aimed at producing an uneven-aged stand. Such a stand presents some possible biological advantages of diversity, but it also presents a most difficult and expensive treatment problem as a result of that same diversity. Treatments favorable to trees of one age class of species may be disastrous to those of another.

In the selection system, only part of the stand is removed. As a result, new growth must be able to survive for an extended period beneath a partial canopy. This is characteristic of climax species and indeed, the selection system most nearly approximates the natural reproduction in a climax forest community. However, there are exceedingly few climax forest stands in the Pacific Northwest and, perhaps because of the frequency of natural disturbance, there never were many. Certainly the old growth forests cut in the past were overwhelmingly *not* climax stands.

In general then, it may be stated that tree species that have a pioneering and intolerant ecological role are favored by harvest methods which create a great deal of disturbance. Clearcutting

131

and seed tree cuttings which leave light cover are such methods. Climax species are favored by shelterwood cuttings in which heavy cover is left, or by selective cuttings. These species require no supplementary treatments.

IMPACTS OF CLEARCUTTING

Stand Health—Methods to prevent and limit the effects of forest diseases and insects are being studied intensively. In the absence of any new information, indications are that clearcutting is the cultural method most likely to prevent or limit diseases and insect attacks. Two disease-related considerations are of paramount importance in planning forest disease control among the species of the Pacific Northwest. First, most forest stands west of the Cascades show the western hemlock component to be heavily infected with dwarf mistletoe. To reproduce hemlock free of dwarf mistletoe, all infected overstory plants must be felled within the diseased area and for 50 feet into the surrounding healthy timber. Past failures to clearcut old growth stands with significant amounts of western hemlock have given rise to new, young stands which are already heavily infected with dwarf mistletoe. Such stands are esthetically unappealing and are economically worthless.

A second consideration relates to the Douglas fir type. When stands of Douglas fir are managed by intermediate cutting methods, the shallow rooting characteristics of these trees predispose the roots to damage. This leaves the stand highly vulnerable to root-rot inducing fungi. For both of these situations, clearcutting is the recommended harvest method.

Wildlife—The removal of the forest canopy, permitting light to reach the forest floor, encourages the growth of shrubs and herbs. The deposition of ash adds a number of elements, especially potassium, in readily available form and thus fertilizes the former understory vegetation. This causes herbaceous and shrubby forage plants to grow in greater profusion and with

132

Old growth presents many hazards, among them dwarf mistletoe infection which may spread (note the bunched, infected branches of old hemlocks), and the bare tops of dead hemlock and Douglas fir which may act as lightning attractors.

Photo, D. Burwell

higher nutritive value than they do in the full canopy forest. The effect of such growth varies with the location and size of the clearcut in question as well as with the needs of the specific wildlife species being considered.

Deer and elk are definitely provided with additional and more nutritious forage after the full canopy forest is clearcut. Where there is a shortage of nutritious forage, as there generally is on the winter range, clearcuts can add to the carrying capacity of the range for these species. To be most effective, winter range clearcuts must be located below the line of deep snow and on slopes with southerly exposures.

Clearcuts on summer range are also used by big game animals, but whether summer range clearcuts contribute materially to big game nutrition remains uncertain. It may be that animals would gain significantly in physical condition in such cut areas. In this way they would have better physical reserves, hence greater survival ability, than otherwise. But the benefit to some is a hardship to other species and the gain for deer and elk in the high country is a loss for woodland caribou which require old-growth forest in which to winter.

Clearcuts ordinarily cause an increase in small mammal populations because of the increased understory growth and the related seed production. This increase would be expected to be reflected in associated predator populations and studies have indicated that this is the case for pine marten. Black bear too are encouraged by the changes associated with clearcutting.

Bird populations are, of course, strongly influenced by clearcutting and by the increased food production provided by invertebrates and fruit. The grouse tribe, especially, has been studied and has been shown to respond favorably to increases in light and warmth on the forest floor.

Fishing—Spawning by adult salmon as well as egg and fry survival of other fresh water species can be influenced by any changes in the quantity and quality of stream flow. Impaired migration may be caused by obstacles such as slash and log

135

A hemlock badly infected with dwarf mistletoe and another already dead of the infection overlook a clearcut of a once heavily-infested area.

Twelve years earlier this area was clearcut to eliminate a dwarf mistletoe infection. Young Douglas fir have sprouted vigorously. Over the next decade these trees will thin themselves out by a process of natural selection. Photo, D. Burwell

jams; decreased permeability of spawning gravel by the addition of sediment. Roads associated with logging have been found to be a major source of such sediment.

In Alaska, where emphasis has been on logging with a minimum of road building and soil disturbance, there have been only small increases in sediment due to logging. In Washington and Oregon, where more roads and tractor skid trails are used, the sediment problem becomes more acute. Sediment affects the oxygen supply around fish embryos and may overcrowd suitable spawning areas by limiting the habitable area available to the fish.

In addition, logging can cause changes in stream temperature, especially during warm periods during the summer. Debris jams can block migrations and cause the deposition of sediment, thereby reducing spawning areas. Where water is sufficiently warm, the decomposition of slash may even release toxic quantities of tannin into the water.

Buffer strips to lessen the impact of logging on streams have often been suggested as a partial solution but the effectiveness of the strips has seldom been measured. The major beneficial effect of buffer strips appears to be that they provide an esthetically pleasing situation to sport fishermen. In general, then, one may conclude that logging, if conducted properly, causes only minimal damage to fish habitat.

Soil-Plant-Water Relationships—Some of the criticism of clear-cutting as a silvicultural practice has been based on the assertion that it contributes substantially to the degradation of the site. Studies of mineral cycling provide some insight into the behavior of west-side forests (west of the Cascades) with regard to plant-soil-water relationships. In general it has been found that there is little in the way of elemental loss by leaching and by erosional processes from these systems.

Although mineral concentrations are affected only minimally by logging, soil moisture and water quantity are affected significantly. Ordinarily stored soil moisture is transpired by

137

plants at the expense of streamflow. Where plant cover is reduced, water yields and resulting streamflows will increase accordingly.

Manipulations of forest cover in the Pacific Northwest may increase water yield in two ways. First, logging can reduce the evapo-transpiration losses during times of maximum stress. This means that streamflow would be increased during dry periods. Second, removal of forest cover in snow zones will cause snow to accumulate preferentially in cleared areas. This, in turn, causes an increased water yield during the time of snow melt.

Another effect which has been noted is that mass movements of land in major earth slippages seem to be correlated with forest harvest operations. During the 1965 Christmas storm, land movements in logged areas of Oregon and southwestern Washington were, indeed, greater than those in unlogged areas. It has not been established, however, whether the slippages were particularly associated with clearcuts or whether they were, in fact, associated with the changed pattern of water movement caused by road construction.

ECONOMIC CONSIDERATIONS

In Washington and Oregon, most federal forest lands are managed by the U.S. Forest Service and by the Bureau of Land Management. In Alaska, most of the forest land from which timber is harvested is national forest, administered by the U.S. Forest Service. Although the BLM has custody of extensive areas in Alaska, most of their lands are not commercial forest lands.

Managing timberlands in southwestern Oregon, the BLM has been moving away from clearcutting. Here they are converting to a three-stage partial cut system which is designed to produce better regeneration on arid south and west slopes than has been obtained in the past.

The U.S. Forest Service, harvesting on the eastern slopes of the Cascades, harvests more than 90 percent of its timber using

138

partial cutting methods. Only in Alaska does the Forest Service clearcut on virtually all national forest areas cut.

A moratorium on clearcutting on federal lands would have both long and short term economic consequences. Many of these would be felt by those sectors of the economy directly engaged in the harvesting and production of timber products. Other consequences would affect those sectors of the economy linked to the forest-based industries in any way.

The exact effect of such a moratorium would depend largely on the particular definition and limitation of "clearcutting" proscribed. Harvesting techniques are not easily segregated into categories, rather they form a broad continuum. Policy measures to restrict cutting practices would have to define precisely which practices were permitted, which prohibited. In addition it would be necessary to specify the category of lands subject to the restrictions.

A ban on clearcutting on all lands would reduce harvest by about 63 percent while a ban on federal lands only would reduce it by approximately 24 percent. Because of the problems of equipment, personnel limitations and increased costs during the first year of a moratorium, only 15 percent of the potential clearcut volume could be harvested by other means. The following residual timber harvest could be expected:

Restrictions	Clearcut Vol. (in millions of board feet)	First Yr.	Second Yr.
On all lands	10,524	1,580	2,631
On federal lands only	4,023	603	1,006

Higher prices could be expected as many operators would be in a position of trying to minimize their short term losses.

Undoubtedly this would lead to a shift in the supply of timber for both the region and the nation. Supplies would come more heavily from parts of the country which do not practice

139

clearcutting as much as the Pacific Northwest—areas such as the Southeast. A ban on cutting on federal lands only would stimulate increased production on non-federal public and on private lands. A ban on clearcutting on all lands would lead to an increase in timber importation from areas such as British Columbia.

Estimates such as these are general and do not identify the impact on specific localized communities and their timber markets. It should be remembered that many communities, particularly in Alaska, are almost entirely dependent on public timber for their economic base.

The effects of a moratorium on clearcutting would also depend on time stipulations in the ban. Because of the lead time required for sale preparation, a prohibition applicable to future sales only would have little immediate impact. Existing contracts would likely sustain many operators for as long as two years. If a moratorium were applied to existing sales as well as to future ones, a substantial reduction in harvest would occur.

For the Douglas fir region (western Oregon and western Washington) it has been estimated that over 44 percent of the manufacturing employment generating sales to markets outside the region originates in the forest products industries. Persons connected with any of these enterprises could be expected to suffer serious economic losses from such a change in policy. Benefits from the reduced harvesting would tend to accrue to a selected sub-group. These individuals who believe that timber should not be harvested or at least should not be clearcut tend to be those who are highly educated and have above-average incomes. To the extent that this is so, there would be a redistribution of economic benefits from the consumer of wood products and the taxpayer, to a select group.

A major economic factor, often overlooked, is the fiscal relationship between the federal government and local and county governments stemming from receipts from public lands. At present, 25 percent of gross receipts from national forest lands are returned to the counties for the support of schools

140

and roads. In Oregon, 75 percent of the receipts from "O and C" lands are returned to the counties, of which one-third (25 percent of the total) is refunded to the BLM for management purposes.

A change in timber harvest would affect these receipts in two ways. First, there would be a reduction in the volume of timber harvested unless a greater area were made available for selective cutting. Second, the average price received for timber would decline, reflecting higher operating costs involved in selective logging. Counties with national forest lands would effectively absorb one-fourth of this reduction while those with "O & C" lands would absorb one-half. This means that a proportionately smaller sum would be passed back to the BLM with the result that the BLM would have considerably reduced funds for management.

Obviously any limitation on clearcutting would have a substantial impact on the economy of the Pacific Northwest. Although a ban might halt clearcutting "mistakes" and inappropriate applications, it would also limit clearcutting on areas where it is reasonable and even necessary. Further, a ban on clearcutting would make it imperative that selective logging be carried out in a vastly increased area in order to maintain the national timber harvest at the current level. With such an increase in area being logged, there is a real potential for major difficulties and it is conceivable that problems now associated with clearcutting would not be overcome, they merely would be shifted to another setting.

ENGINEERING CONSIDERATIONS

Most logging in the Pacific Northwest is carried out by some form of the system known as cable logging. In a cable system, a wire rope is stretched from a log concentration site called a "landing" into the forest where the felling and bucking take place. These cables haul the logs out of the forest to the landing. Once at the landing, logs are loaded onto trucks for the longer haul to the mill. The precise configurations of the cable systems determine, in part, the amount of road which is needed for that long haul.

In general, cable systems—both high lead and skyline—are readily adapted to clearcut harvesting. They tend to develop geometrical cutting boundaries but with modifications they have been used to produce irregular and blended cut areas.

In recent years, spectacular new developments in cable logging have come to promise increased versatility for the system. In balloon logging, a modification of the traditional high lead system, a tethered balloon is substituted for the single steel spar which supports the cable at the landing. The balloon raises the logs off the ground completely and moves them to the landing in the manner of the conventional skyline which boasts two spars, one at either end of the line.

Where cable logging is not indicated, a mobile tractor yarding system is frequently employed. In such a system, a tractor drives to the site of felling and bucking, picks up the logs at one end and drags them to the deck. This system requires a network of long haul truck roads just as does cable logging but, in addition, it requires the construction of a series of short haul tractor trails which extend from the landing into the forest. In general, tractor logging is indicated where partial cutting methods are used, while clearcutting is usually associated with cable system harvesting. Tractor logging is used primarily on the east side of the Washington and Oregon Cascades, while cable logging dominates the west slopes and Alaska.

Another system, neither cable nor tractor, is presently being studied seriously although it is still somewhat experimental. This is helicopter logging, a system in which large helicopters pick logs out of the forest and carry them to the appointed concentration sites. Whether this system is a practical alternative to the two major systems now in use remains to be demonstrated.

From an ecological vantage point, the main impact of harvesting on the forest is in the construction of roads. Roads

142

One of the earliest models of balloon logging brings a log to the landing. Balloon logging, if successful, will make possible logging without soil disturbance as well as logging in areas of difficult access.

cause site disturbances. They contribute to erosion and subsequent siltation and they cause soil compaction which affects run-off and makes regeneration difficult.

The road systems developed for tractor logging differ qualitatively from those developed for cable logging. In general, cable logging systems pull logs uphill, hence the road system associated with cable logging is designed to get to the ridges as quickly as possible and to stay there. Tractor logging, on the other hand, is downhill logging. Its primary roads follow stream bottoms while its secondary roads and tractor trails cut across the hills connecting primary roads with each other. The amount of road required is also a function of the size of the cut for a road must touch each harvest unit. The greater the area involved in logging, the more road is required to reach it unless the area is clearcut. Where clearcutting is employed, the ratio of road mileage varies inversely with the size of the clearcut.

The relative merits of tractor vs. cable logging must be evaluated in light of other considerations than merely the number of miles of road created. With either system, the impact of the road systems on streams can be great or small. If roads have proper bridges and culverts at stream crossings, the impact on streamflow and siltation can be minimized. If construction is carried out improperly, the impact is immense. As tractor logging requires a much larger number of stream crossings than cable logging, its potential for stream damage is greater. This is one inherent problem which must be considered in the selection of logging method.

Another problem is that of compaction. The compaction of the forest floor caused by extensive tractor movement is a more severe disturbance than the abrasive action of logs dragging over the forest floor which is characteristic of a high lead operation. Where skyline logging is employed, logs are lifted free of the ground and the impact on the soil is truly minimal. At the present time, most foresters believe that site damage due to road construction and to the compaction caused by tractor yarding exceeds the disturbance caused by cable systems. Thus in logging its watershed, Seattle has specified high lead logging of clearcuts as its preferred method of harvest—and the city insists on yarding distances one-third longer than normal to reduce truck road mileage.

Tractor and cable logging differ too in their effect on buffer strips. It is becoming common practice in the Northwest to protect stream beds by leaving buffer strips. As cable systems yard uphill, they make the preservation of buffer strips easy. Tractor logging with its associated cross hill yarding, makes it more difficult to maintain banks and buffer strips inviolate.

ESTHETIC CONSIDERATIONS

The choice of harvesting methods is hard to assess when considering esthetics for what is attractive to one may be anathema to another. One thing is certain however—minimal ecological impact does not always coincide with maximum beauty, at least not with beauty in the conventionally accepted sense.

Clearcutting has relatively great impact, yet it has been practiced without esthetically displeasing results in many countries. It is even accepted practice on areas as esthetically sensitive as the slopes of Mt. Fujiyama, Japan's most sacred shrine. There are many preservationists, however, who feel that as clearcutting is more visible than partial cutting, it is necessarily esthetically less desirable. Unfortunately, to force partial cut silviculture in situations in which clearcutting is clearly a better biological forestry practice, is to court ecological disaster under the cover of esthetics.

PROBLEMS OF PARTIAL CUTTING

The problems inherent in partial cutting are numerous. Partial cutting systems would increase sale preparation costs as men and time are required to select and mark trees to be retained. More forest land would be needed to provide a given volume of

timber and harvesting disturbance on any given area would be more frequent. Harvest exclusively by partial cut methods would require as much as 120 percent more road miles per square mile of forest than is needed under the present system, and the sudden acceleration of road building activity caused by such a shift could double the cost of the roads.

Partial cuts also present silvicultural difficulties as they reduce flexibility in felling and yarding and they require exceptional care to avoid damage to reserved trees. Where natural regeneration is successful, regeneration costs would be low on partially cut areas but where natural regeneration failed, brush control and planting programs would be very expensive.

Increased blowdown losses, damage to residual stands caused by decay and disease, reduced opportunities for salvage and reduced growth would all combine to lower the amount of timber which could be harvested from the forest under this system. In general it is likely that yields from the forests would be reduced considerably under partial cutting methods of harvest.

CONCLUSION

A study of the role of clearcutting as a forestry practice indicates that there is historical precedent for its use as a sound management tool and that it is widely used in the Pacific Northwest. It is also clear that the propriety of using clearcutting as a harvesting method varies widely from region to region and indeed from site to site within a region.

Methods of harvesting are being changed and improved, but this is a slow process and involves use and obsolescence of expensive capital equipment. As the timber stand in the West changes from an old growth to a second and third harvest, silvicultural methods and the accompanying harvest techniques must change as well.

Decisions with respect to forest management on public lands are a function not only of timber growing and harvesting

147

A lush thicket of manzanita grows up quickly after a clearcut on the western slopes of Oregon's Cascade Mountains.

requirements but also of other uses. As the role of various uses change in the management of a forest, the practices employed by foresters in the conduct of that management also change. Forestry decisions are long term decisions, whereas public moods and views as reflected in pressures on legislative and administrative public officials may vary on short term cycles.

Precipitous decisions on long term forest management practice which are responsive to short term changes in public pressures can have profound effects upon forest land use, the cost and availability of timber supply and the economic health of the nation and specifically on regions and communities that are forest dependent.

It is clear that much research is required to obtain answers to many of the questions raised in the current debate. This research should be designed to illuminate the trade-offs inherent in multiple use of forest land. If the questions being raised concerning forest land use are to be resolved, it will be necessary for the nation to undertake a large research program to study the behavior of managed forest ecosystems of the sort that is being pursued with respect to natural forest systems under the International Biological Program. It is urged that such a coordinated study be undertaken in the various forest regions of the nation.

7

Hubbard Brook Revisited

DEEP IN THE WHITE MOUNTAINS OF New Hampshire, the U.S. Forest Service maintains one of its many forest research facilities; the now famous Hubbard Brook Experimental Forest. Here, some years ago a team of investigators undertook to study the course of water and minerals through a forest by stripping away the vegetation. Thus began one of the most significant experiments involving the clearing of a forest; one which has been used by preservationists to condemn all clearcutting. No look at clearcutting could be complete without a glance at what was done in this cut.

From the experimentalist's point of view, Hubbard Brook is a superb place to locate a comparative study. The forest is made up of several small, discrete watersheds, and on six of these, biological, chemical and hydrological data have been gathered for many years. The six watersheds vary in size but they are basically quite similar to each other. All six share the same continental climate; all have steep slopes and southern exposures. The soils of the six all developed from the same coarse, glacial till—thus experimental results gained on any one watershed could legitimately be compared with similar measurements from any of the other five watersheds.

A most important characteristic shared by the six watersheds is that they all lie over a layer of impermeable quartz-based bedrock. The bedrock is about 5 feet below the surface and no water can seep through it. Thus any water falling into the area must either be used by plants in the processes of growth or transpiration and thus be returned to the atmosphere, or it must run off the watershed into the adjacent stream. There is essentially no ground water storage. Here then is a unique setting in which investigators could measure how much water was taken up by a forest; water would either be transpired by the vegetation or it would appear in the streamflow. As precipitation and streamflow are easily measured and as the amount of water used in growth is negligible compared to the amount used in transpiration, it remained merely to subtract the one from the other to determine the amount used in evapotranspiration. This may effectively be expressed as Precipitation—Streamflow = Transpired water.

One of the aims of the experiments at Hubbard Brook was to measure this quantity so that investigators could find out precisely how much streamflow there would be if virtually none of the water were intercepted by vegetation. Interest in this problem had grown as it was noted that growing populations were placing increasing pressure on relatively limited water supplies, especially during summer months when streamflow tends to be at a minimum. How much, it was wondered, could the yield of a watershed be increased by reducing transpiration losses? And if the water yield could be increased significantly, would this affect flood flows at peak times? Would it affect the quality of the water coming off the watershed?

To find out, drastic measures were required. The hillsides would have to be laid bare and kept so for a prolonged period while measurements were taken. Such methods would never be suggested as forms of forest management for they were designed to impede regeneration—precisely the opposite aim of sound forest management. No one could, does or would manage a forest in this way except for experimental purposes; the methods are far too severe.

In December of 1965 crews began the task of denuding one of the six watersheds, Watershed #2. Within the month woody vegetation in the 39 acre watershed was cut. The felled material

150

was left to decompose on the ground. This, after all, was a water yield and mineral study. There was no need to "harvest" the wood. By leaving the felled material the investigators were able to avoid the confounding effects of logging roads and of associated soil disturbances.

In spring when non-woody plants and young shoots began to grow again it became apparent that it would be necessary to eliminate them. To this end the entire experimental area was sprayed with a powerful herbicide. Soon the remnants of ground cover were dead; and the shoots had withered. Each summer throughout the experimental period—1966, 1967, 1968—the area had to be defoliated to prevent regrowth. With the vegetation successfully eliminated it was possible to measure streamflow and water quality and to observe what would happen without the forest on that particular hillside.

What were the results? At first no change was apparent for the winter months are dormant months for trees of the New England forest. During those months the forest has virtually no effect on the water passing by it. By June, five months after the initial cutting, the trees were beginning to grow again. This was the time of the first spraying. It was also the time when the changes in the water regime became evident.

The biggest change was in the amount of water which left the area as streamflow. 40% more water ran off the cleared watershed each year than ran off the adjacent forested watersheds. This change was brought about by eliminating transpiration by forest vegetation. Predictably the change in streamflow was most evident during the growing months, June to September. From October to May, when the trees would have been dormant, total flow was affected very little.

The timing of this increase in waterflow was of interest to the research team for it showed incontrovertibly that any rise in streamflow caused by elimination of vegetation would change primarily the summer flows. These are flows which are usually low at a time when the demand for water is high and the risk of possible flooding from an excess of water is negligible.

151

Watershed No. 2, Hubbard Brook Experimental Forest, showed up very clearly during snow time while it was kept free of trees. Here it is seen from Route 93, Campton, N.H.

152

Floodtime in New England occurs at the time of snowmelt and here again it was wondered whether clearing the watershed could help. Snow on the cleared area, it was observed, melted a few days before snow on the surrounding wooded areas. Thus, snowmelt time could be desynchronized by cutting. The effect was small however, and it was deemed too slight to alter flood patterns unless vast areas were cleared simultaneously.

Water quality, a factor of considerable concern, showed a distinct change for the worse during the experimental years.

As light and heat became more abundant at the erstwhile forest floor, and as they combined with an increase in available water, the rate of decomposition of the organic layers of the forest floor soared. Nutrients were released from the rotting vegetation and, as there were no plants remaining to utilize these nutrients, they were washed away into the stream and carried out of the watershed. Nitrates were found in especially large concentrations reaching peak levels of 60 ppm the first year and 80 ppm the second year—well above the 45 ppm level considered safe for human consumption. Other major nutrients such as calcium, potassium, sodium, and magnesium were found at concentrations 3 to 20 times their normal levels.

Annual sediment losses or more precisely particulate matter that reached the streams from eroded banks and disturbed channels were about 9 times the normal losses.

The excess sunlight and heat in the cleared area also affected the temperature of the stream. Enriched by the extra nitrates and warmed by the additional sunlight, the waters came to support dense colonies of algae not found in streams draining undisturbed forests.

Although the application of herbicides was discontinued after the 1968 growing season, vegetative regrowth during the next summer (1969) was severely retarded apparently by the residual effects of the herbicide. Thus the watershed response in 1969 to water quantity and quality was similar to that during the period of treatment.

153

In the summer of 1970 vegetation began to recover from the repressive herbicide and become established throughout the watershed. Natural regrowth from several sources provided the regeneration—seed stored in the humus layers of the soil, seed blown or carried in from the edge of the adjacent undisturbed forest, sprouts from tree stumps that were repeatedly killed back by repeated herbicide applications, and a few plants that were unaffected by the herbicide. After 4 growing seasons the watershed has a lush growth of pin cherry (a pioneer species), some beech, maple, and white ash sprouts, a few yellow birch seedlings along with other shrubs (mainly raspberry), and herbs.

Along with the gradual vegetative regrowth during each successive summer, streamflow has progressively diminished. This decline in streamflow has come about because of increased transpiration—more vegetation generally means greater transpiration.

Streamflow, that initially increased to 40% greater than in the uncut forest, was reduced to levels equal to the adjacent uncut forest within 4 years after the last spraying.

Nutrient concentrations in stream water also returned to pretreatment levels after 4 years. Nitrate levels for example now seldom exceed 2 ppm and are usually less than 0.1 ppm during the summer months. Particulate matter in the streams also has reached pretreatment levels.

In summary, the experiment conducted at Hubbard Brook indicates that unquestionably forest vegetation has a profound effect on the quality and quantity of water passing through the area. A drastic treatment—in this case *total* deforestation and virtual devegetation—can have many far-reaching consequences. Water quality can be damaged and a sizeable volume of nutrients may be drained from the forest ecosystem. But the study also underlines the extreme resilience of the forest—it is an ecosystem which regenerates rapidly despite the most severe disturbance. Eight years after this super devastating "clearcut"—which was not an experiment in forest practice but in hydrology—Hubbard Brook forest is virtually back to

154

normal. This ability of the healthy forest to "bounce back" is an extremely important protective mechanism for both forest sites and streams and it is vital in any consideration of forest cutting and regrowth.

8 | Clearcutting and Economics

by
Ernest M. Gould, Jr.
Forest Economist
Harvard University

THE ROMAN DEITY JANUS is always shown with one face looking back and one forward. Economists often seem two-faced also when they tackle a problem about the future by first looking to see how similar situations worked out in the past. In an uncertain future, history seldom repeats itself but experience does help us think about what may happen.

Since settlement began on this continent most of our harvested forests have been clearcut, so it may be useful to see why. In the first place farmers wanted to turn woods into fields, and clearcutting was the only way to get sunlight down to the soil so crops would grow. Then, the only economic question was how best to get rid of the trees. Later on, permanent woodlots also were clearcut, but only in patches big enough to get next winter's fuel. Although concentrating the cut in a small area made the work easier for men and oxen, here and there some promising trees were left to grow big enough for the boards needed around the farm.

In the 1800's large scale lumbering got underway in the still unsettled old growth forests of Maine and clearcut areas got bigger. Because all the useable trees on a tract were cut at one time, the size and shape of a clearcut area depended on the distribution of big timber. In the northeast, new trees much like the old ones sprang up almost immediately, but few businessmen could afford to wait for them to mature. So loggers moved on to other regions where there was a seemingly endless supply

156

of virgin forest on public land that could be bought for a song. As long as there were trees ready for the axe just over the hill, it didn't make financial sense to try and grow them from scratch, especially when the full grown trees cost only a fraction of what it would take to bring a seedling to maturity on cut-over land.

For a time this system served the needs of the country surprisingly well. Many people wanted to get out of the crowded east, and the federal decision to give away or to sell our western lands cheaply made rapid expansion possible. Farmers got land, lumbermen got standing timber and the treasury got some money. The combination of clearcutting, large-scale milling and low rail rates brought lumber to the settlers in abundance. Competition kept prices low so that new farms, towns and cities sprang up like mushrooms. Some of the cut-over land became farms, and the rest sooner or later produced another crop of trees.

The political decision to dispose of the public domain quickly greatly stimulated lumbermen to market the wood consumers needed at prices they could afford. Thus public and private action combined to speed the settlement of the West, which created a market for eastern industrial output and grew the food needed in cities and for export to Europe. Thus guided by law and the market, the nation's economy grew rapidly.

However, there were serious flaws in the system. Some very large personal fortunes were made by "timber barons," which suggests that the public may have gotten too little for its forest land. Cheap timber also encouraged the lumber industries to "cut and get out," leaving behind the social costs of a string of ghost towns and bankrupt communities. When the mills moved out, the owners of many small businesses and homes were stranded and lost everything as the bottom dropped out of values. Near the turn of the century some spectacular forest fires on cut-over land in the Lake States finished off what was left of some localities and for miles around set regeneration back a generation. Public attention was gripped by these holocausts, and for the first time people saw some of the social costs that rapid exploitation can impose on a donor area. Neither the political system nor the market system was then prepared to cooperate and compensate the loosers.

Luckily, time was ripe for a change because the bottom of the land barrel was in sight. After cutting over the Northeast, the Lake States and the South, there was no place left to go but the Northwest. It was apparent that the supply of cheap timber on public land that had fueled the system till now was running out.

The scanty statistics on hand during the last decades of the 1800's showed that the lumber cut each year was greater than the estimated growth in the virgin forests of the West and the second growth forests of the East and South. Many concluded that overcutting would eventually deplete our stock of timber if we didn't use less, find wood substitutes or somehow get more production out of our forests.

Foresters were ready with a proposal to increase production, and some rather remarkable characters like Gifford Pinchot started to vigorously promote the idea that trees could be economically cropped like other plants so that any forest property could produce a continuous flow of timber. In addition, they said that the government should keep its unsold forest land and manage it for a sustained yield of the products that the economy would certainly need. Furthermore, private owners should do the same because wood from their lands would be needed too.

New political rules were adopted to stop the sale of some of the best of the remaining public forest land and to set it up as National Forests which could be managed for timber and water in perpetuity. However, Congress never accepted the idea of regulating the use of private forest land, so the market system has continued to direct the use of these resources largely unfettered, except in those states that have set up minimum forest practice standards.

At the early propaganda stage, forests said they could provide the timber needed to provision the economy and at the same time maintain the stable communities so much desired by rural folk. A sort of shorthand jargon developed in which scientific forestry was epitomized by the term "selective cutting" and all the evils of exploitation by "clearcutting." The public remembered that clearcutting is anathema long after all the other details were forgotten. So it's not surprising that foresters are now flayed when it turns out that for some time they have been quietly clearcutting large areas on the National Forests. Many people wonder if this represents a return to the old "cut and get out" system which obviously won't work now that forest land is limited in supply.

An added cause for concern is the fact that consumer demands have changed drastically. Now that most of us live in cities we need woodland more than ever before for outdoor recreation and esthetic satisfactions. Also, we use pure water in quantities that are hard to imagine, and forests play a useful role in providing it. Even the capacity of trees to use up carbon dioxide from the air and return oxygen may make a significant improvement in air quality. Altogether, there are a host of benefits society realizes from forests besides wood and most of them are not bought and sold in any market.

It is a fact of modern life that these "public goods" are often worth more than timber products in forests near urban areas, and their development cannot be left to a market system which doesn't evaluate them. With more people we need more of every forest value, and it is a moot question how we should manage our available land to serve all purposes. But it seems clear that we need some new balance to control the interplay between the political system and the market system if we are to use forest resources to our greatest advantage.

Part of the answer about how to manage our forests in the future depends on the role we assign to clearcutting. A good deal of our present harvesting is done this way, and we must assess the effects of any proposed change. Once the biological and engineering effects are straightened out, economic impacts can be studied. Unfortunately, economists can't give simple answers because they know that in the short-run things often work out differently than they do in the long-run, and both are important. Also there are at least three important points of view that must be considered—the likely impact of a proposed change on the smallest producing unit, the firm; the way innovations affect the larger economy beyond the firm; and finally the way the welfare of individuals will change.

We can start at the bottom with a small logging company and see how the repercussions of a shift from clearcutting to some form of partial-harvest cutting might work out. Let's look first at the reaction of the manager when he heard recently that the President might suddenly order a moratorium on clearcutting.

Let's say that he was the high bidder to clearcut one hundred acres of National Forest land in the west containing an estimated five million board feet. He agreed to pay $75 for each thousand board feet of logs he actually cuts, in addition to building ten miles of road that meets Forest Service standards to get in and out of the sale area. He also has a contract to deliver the logs to a sawmill which will pay him $125 per thousand board feet. With all these contractual arrangements necessary to his livelihood, he is likely to be very upset by any idea of a sudden change; he has enough uncertainties to cope with without adding one more. Of course, he'd soon find out that the proposed moratorium only applies to new sales, and that present contracts will go ahead as planned.

This will relieve his mind considerably, but he will start thinking about how he can operate in the future if clearcutting is out and partial-cutting is in. He knows that on the ground the logging situation will get more complicated when some trees have to be left behind in good condition to grow. Choppers can no longer fell trees simply so that they can be removed handily. They will have to drop trees in ways that minimize damage to the residual stand. This may make skidding the trees or logs to a roadside more difficult, and greater care will have to be taken not to damage standing trees in the process. Altogether, partial-harvesting takes more time and trouble than clearcutting;

160

he may conclude that it will be necessary to buy new logging equipment better suited to the more meticulous job. He will also have to retrain his men in some new skills. There is little doubt that at first, cutting and skidding costs will rise while he is getting geared up to the new harvest methods.

In addition, road building will also cost more because now it will be necessary to cover more ground to cut the same amount of timber. If about half the trees are left to grow, then about twice as many acres must be worked over each year. The main access road may be about the same in either case, so road length will not double, but the increase will be substantial. The same would be true if ten 10-acre plots were clearcut instead of one 100-acre tract. In addition, because the same road may be used later for the final harvest, it may have to be built better than for a single clearcut, and this costs the logger more.

The road problem is important to everyone because the chief source of erosion during and after logging of any kind is road wash. The simple act of removing a tree has little effect on the forest floor where accumulated litter stops overground flow and helps rain soak into the soil. But in steep terrain woods, roads must be well designed, carefully built and maintained to prevent erosion.

One effect of more roads will be to create a larger number of scars on the landscape, thus reducing its esthetic appeal. In mountainous country where slopes are visible for miles around, additional roads may reduce public satisfaction much more than in flat terrain where one has to be practically on top of a road in order to see it.

With all these changes, our logger will almost certainly expect his operating costs to go up when he can no longer clearcut. He will therefore want to pay the Forest Service less for stumpage next time, or get paid more for his logs at the mill. Sealed competitive bidding for stumpage will probably make him afraid to lower his offer to buy standing trees, so he is most likely to ask for more money at the sawmill. In times like these when the demand for construction lumber is brisk, he will

161

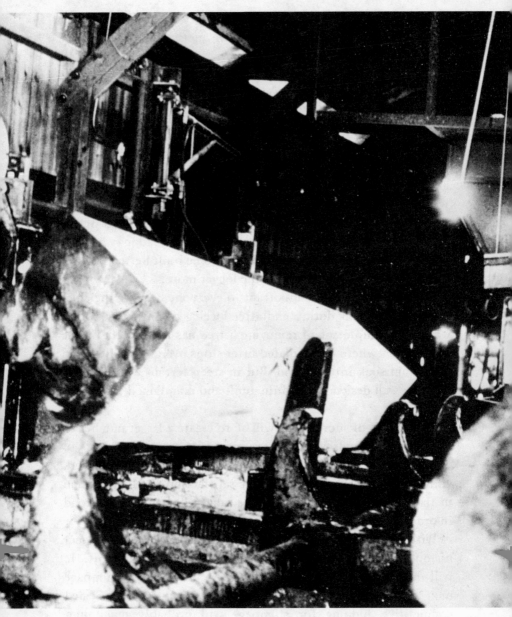

In the short run, partial-cutting will undoubtedly raise prices at the sawmill.

Photo, P. A. Vohs, Jr.

probably get it. Because the milling and transportation of lumber is already rather well organized, there isn't much chance that the mill can increase its efficiency enough to offset the extra charge for logs. Consequently, the mill is very likely to pass on the extra cost through the channels of trade to the consumers of housing and other wood products.

There is little doubt that in the short-run abandoning clearcutting will increase costs throughout the economy. Eventually the consumer will pay the difference in higher costs for the things that he buys. This can bear most heavily on the poor whose welfare is already low. In addition, scenic costs to the public at large may mount together with some adverse effects on water quality and other social values.

We must look ahead a bit longer to take account of the costs of regenerating the forest. In the humid East, trees will generally cover an area in a year or two, regardless of the way it was cut, so that the landscape looks green again and watershed conditions are restored. In the more arid parts of the country, west of the 100th meridian, delays may be longer. But even here, with good management and a bit of luck, five years will restock the land with trees.

However, there will always be some areas where natural seeding fails, often due to wild fires, and artificial seeding or planting is needed. This extra work will be undertaken on public land, and on most industrial holdings now that companies have settled down to manage their lands. Every citizen has a stake in seeing that such failures are kept to minimum because they eventually pay the bills for restoration either through higher taxes or product prices. In addition, until failed areas heal over they usually yield less of the several social values.

A decade or so later there may be gains that can help offset the higher short-run cost of using partial cutting instead of clearcutting. The more elaborate road net can facilitate fire suppression, insect and disease control, and help the prompt salvage of natural losses. It can also make possible improvement

cuttings and thinnings that otherwise don't yield enough to pay for a special road. In general, roads may promote more intensive management which can raise the productivity of responsive forest land. This in turn could reduce the pressure to cut on other lands that are most valuable for those social values that are not compatible with timber management. Finally, when the trees left behind in the first partial-harvest cutting are ready to cut, new roads will not be needed thus lowering logging costs. Of course, some of these savings will be used up in maintaining a larger permanent road system, but there should be a net social gain.

If we look ahead even farther, another picture emerges, because we may be approaching the end of an era as several long-term trends converge to create a new forest future. The controversy over clearcutting is likely to be lost in the broader problem of managing all our resources in ways that will give more people an acceptable life style.

Past predictions of a timber famine in the United States have not materialized for a combination of reasons that are not likely to be repeated. First, the information about forests was in error so that we had more than expected, and growth was greater than predicted. Second, our use of wood per capita has declined steadily. This drop in individual consumption has been so great that we now use about the same total amount of wood as we did in 1900, in spite of having about three times as many people and five times as big an economy. Lumber has stayed about the same while the declines in fuelwood, poles, ties and the like have released enough wood to take care of the tremendous increase in paper, plywood and chip board consumption. These changing product trends seem likely to continue. Third, we import an increasing amount of the wood we need from abroad, especially from the underused areas of Canada. Fourth, we have stopped using wood for a great many things which are better made from metal, plastic, ceramics, and the like. Finally, continuous forest management is now the rule rather than the exception on industrial as well as public land. Except for some

Like a row crop, seedlings grow in Weyerhaeuser Company nurseries. Where natural seeding fails, artificial seeding or planting is necessary. Seedlings will be transplanted by machine and by hand to regenerate the forestlands. Photo, P. A. Vohs, Jr.

operators too small to be interested in continuity, it doesn't pay to cut and get out. Most of these changes are not easily reversed even if it were desirable.

These trends combine to suggest that in the future forests will bear a relatively lighter part of the load of supporting the material needs of our economy. And we will likely manage our land more intensively to produce necessary supplies.

This relatively optimistic outlook must be modified by another set of events. First, it is apparent that an urban industrial civilization puts considerable strain on the natural environment which increases its demand for the ameliorating social values of forest land. Seldom can all of these values be produced from the same acre so we will have to be very ingenious in finding new management practices that reduce the conflicts between uses, or we will unnecessarily lose some production from a good deal of forest land. Many people and agencies are working to solve this kind of problem, but we need the results as soon as possible. More effort is required before we get locked into unsound land-use schemes.

Second, city people are continually buying up forest land for camps and second homes. This often breaks large holdings into many small tracts which are not suited for forest management. Unfortunately many of the new owners are unskilled and uninterested in producing timber or any of the social values for the public. As significant amounts of land are neutralized this way, it may be necessary to make some new political decisions to influence management by private owners. Because the market system doesn't seem to prevent this or any of the other deleterious effects of urban sprawl, a change is needed to insure the supply to the public of the forest values we need.

Perhaps the biggest unknown is the influence that rising world affluence and the freer international movement of goods and services is having on the distribution of global resources. The current situation with oil and food illustrates how closely knit together the world's resources now are. It is apparent that the United States can no longer steer a course independent of other nations. The highly developed nations can now outbid us in world markets, and we depend on others for much of the raw material that supplies our industrial complex. The total pressure of rising living standards everywhere is increasing the drain on world resources so that our old position of dominance is probably gone forever. This shift in economic power has probably permanently raised the prices we pay for all our everyday things. Eventually this will change our life style.

In the long-run the world wide pressure on all resources should reinforce our political and economic incentives to manage forest land more intensively, because forests are renewable and can be continuously cropped. The simultaneous need for more social values from forests, and a heightened concern for a high quality environment will force managers to be more sensitive to public needs. More complex management cannot help but raise costs, but with luck the returns to individuals and society will more than pay off in a higher level of human welfare more equitably distributed to all people.

Glossary

Buck—To cut a felled tree into log lengths.

Cat—Caterpillar tractor, used to drag or skid logs to the deck.

Climax Association—A community of plants, usually named for the dominant species, which grows after a series of other plant groups have succeeded each other. This culminating stage is more stable than the preceding stages although it too may be altered by changes in the environment. The specific nature of any given climax association is determined by climate, soil, terrain and surrounding vegetation.

Edaphic—Related to soil or topography rather than climate.

Epicormic—Arising from a dormant bud on the stem or branch of a woody plant; hence an epicormic branch is one which arises from a section of otherwise clear, unknotted timber.

Fall—To cut down as a tree. (Participle) falling, *e.g.*, falling a tree. Faller—one who cuts trees.

Fell—Variation of *to fall*; more frequently used by persons other than loggers.

High Lead—A system of yarding in which a tall metal spar is erected at the landing or a tall tree at the landing is designated as spar. A steel cable is stretched from the spar to a tree in the forest. From this cable, short cables called chokers are dropped to the logged area. One end of the choker is connected to one end of a log. This end of the log is then raised off the ground so that the log is pulled to the landing with only the butt end dragging on the ground. This method produces less soil disturbance than does yarding in which the total length and weight of a log remains on the ground while the log is dragged to the landing.

Intolerant—Not able to grow in shade; needing direct sunlight for proper growth.

Landing—A collection station where logs, felled and bucked in the forest, are gathered and held until they are removed to market.

Log Deck—see *Landing*.

O & C Lands—Lands at one time granted to the Oregon and Coos Bay Wagon Road development group. The original purpose of the grant was to induce construction and development of the western area and the land grant was similar to grants made, at that time, to railroad companies. As the Oregon-Coos Bay road was never built, the granted lands reverted to federal ownership. At present these timber rich lands are divided between the Forest Service and the Bureau of Land Management.

Seed Tree Harvest—A method of harvest in which almost all of the trees on a given area are cut while a selected few well-spaced, fertile and mature trees (ca. 4/acre) are left to produce seed for a new stand. This method is used where the intention is to allow natural reseeding rather than planting to restock the area.

Selective Cutting—A system of harvest in which foresters examine the area to be logged and mark trees of a particular species, size or condition. Only trees so marked are felled in the subsequent logging operation. These trees are then removed around other trees which have been left standing. The remaining trees may (as in a weeding cut) or may not (as in highgrading) be cut at a later date.

Serotinous—Coming late. Serotinous species are those which bear flowers or fruit late in the season. Serotinous cones are those which remain on the tree, unopened, for one or more years. In forestry the term is commonly associated with species such as jack pine, whose cones do not ordinarily open without fire or other intense heat.

Shelterwood—A cutting system in which the majority of trees in a given area are harvested at one time while some large trees (ca. 13/acre) are left standing to provide wind shelter for young trees of the following generation. These sheltering trees may be cut once reproduction is firmly established, usually a few years after the original cut.

Skid—To move logs from the place in which they were felled to a central location where they may be stored temporarily. Skidding implies that the logs so moved are moved over the surface of the ground.

Skyline Logging—A system of yarding in which two metal spars are erected at topographically high points at opposite ends of the section of forest which has been cut. The spars are connected by a steel cable called the skyline. Choker cables extend from the skyline to the ground. Logs attached to these chokers are lifted clear of the ground and are transported to the landing without touching the ground.

Silvic—Pertaining to the culture and cultivation of trees especially to matters of health and growth.

Tolerant—Able to grow under conditions in which sunlight is scarce, *e.g.*, in the shade of larger trees.

Yard (in logging)—To collect logs at a central location or landing for leading and transport to a mill. Yarding is usually performed over the surface of the ground by a *cat* or cable system *e.g., high lead*. Logs may, however, be yarded well above the ground by *skyline*, balloon or helicopter.

Yard (in wildlife management)—A small, cleared area in which animals such as deer concentrate during periods of harsh, especially snowy, weather. Also, the act of aggregating in an unduly small area. Where yarding behavior persists for a prolonged period, animals may overeat their food supply and starve rather than seek for food outside the yard.

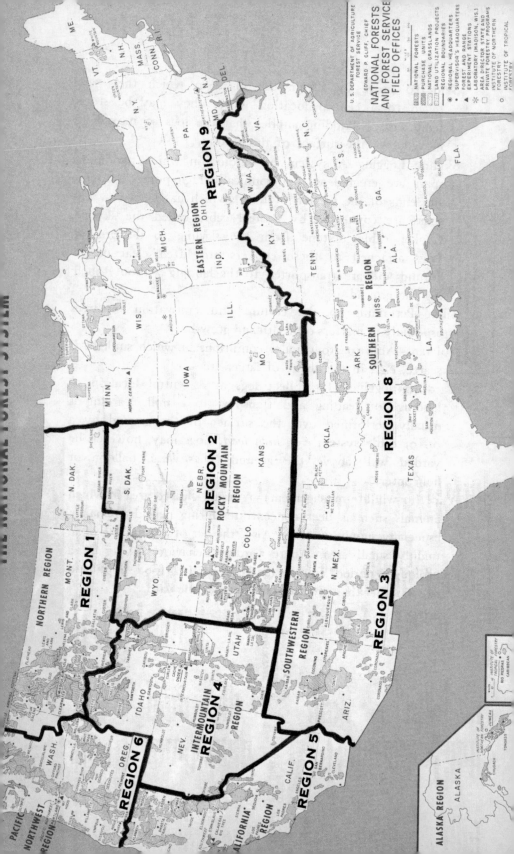

Bibliography

The following list of readings has been gathered to help the reader who may wish to obtain more information on forest management and its related controversies. The items listed here have been selected for general interest and readability. A few take strong positions and have been included as representative of such presentations. A few are technical in nature but have been included because of their importance. These latter have been designated "T."

1. *American Forests*—The magazine of the American Forestry Assn. 1319 18th Street, N.W., Washington, D.C. 20036.
2. Aubertin, G.M., and J.H. Patric 1972 "Quality Water from Clearcut Forest Land?" Northern Logger & Timber Processor 20(8):14-15, 22-23. T
3. Barkley, Paul W., and David W. Seckler 1972 *Economic Growth and Environmental Decay* Harcourt, Brace, Jovanovich, New York. T
4. Connaughton, C.A. 1970 "The Revolt Against Clearcutting" *Journal of Forestry* 68:264-265.
5. Frome, Michael 1971 *The Forest Service* Praeger Publishers, New York.
6. Hewlett, J.D. & J.E. Douglas 1968 "Blending Forest Uses" U.S. Forest Service Southeastern Forest Experiment Station Research Paper SE37.

7. Industrial Publications—A variety of publications relating to clearcutting and other forest practices are available from:

> Industrial Forestry Assn.
> 1410 S.W. Morrison St.
> Portland, Oregon 97205
>
> National Forest Products Assn.
> 1619 Massachusetts Ave. N.W.
> Washington, D.C. 20036
>
> Western Wood Products Assn.
> 1500 Yeon Building
> Portland, Oregon 97204.

8. Likens, G.E., F.H. Borman, N.H. Johnson, D.W. Fisher and R.S. Pierce 1970 "Effects of Forest Cutting and Herbicide Treatment on Nutrient Budgets in the Hubbard Brook Watershed Ecosystem" Ecological Monographs 40:23-47. T

9. McCormick, Jack 1967 *The Life of the Forest* McGraw-Hill, New York.

10. Malone, Joseph J. 1965 *Pine Trees and Politics* Univ. of Washington Press, Seattle.

11. Marquis, D.A. 1967 "Clearcutting in Northern Hardwoods: Results After 30 Years" U.S. Forest Service Northeastern Forest Experiment Station Research Paper NE-85. T

12. Reidel, C.H. 1971 "Environment: New Imperatives for Forest Policy" *Journal of Forestry* 69(5):266-270.

13. Schiff, Ashley L. 1962 *Fire & Water, Scientific Heresy in the Forest Service* Harvard Univ. Press, Cambridge.

14. Shaw, Elmer W. 1970 "Pro and Con Analysis of Clearcutting as a Forestry Practice in the United States" Legislative Reference Service of the Library of Congress Report 70-191EP, Washington, D.C.

15. Thomson, Betty 1958 *The Changing Face of New England* MacMillan, N.Y.

16. U.S. Department of Agriculture Yearbook 1949 *Trees,* Washington, D.C.
17. U.S. Senate 1972 "Clearcutting on Federal Timberlands" A report of the Subcommittee on Public Lands to the Committee on Interior and Insular Affairs

    also

    "Clearcutting Practices on National Timberlands"—A transcript of the hearings before the Senate subcommittee on Public Lands, Washington, D.C.
18. Wood, Nancy 1971 *Clearcut* A Sierra Club Battlebook, San Francisco.

Poorly designed roads pose a serious threat to forest streams and are a major source of erosion. As seen here, the problem is equally severe—if less visible—on selectively logged areas as on clearcuts.

Index

179.

Other Acropolis Books on Current Issues:

University of Maryland Distinguished Lecture Series
THE POLITICAL IMAGE MERCHANTS
Strategies in the New Politics
Edited by Ray Hiebert, Robert Jones, Ernest Lotito, and John Lorenz
With forewords by Rogers C.B. Morton, Robert J. Dole and Lawrence O'Brien

Was the 1972 election the mostly intensely *canned* television campaign in history? Was the person you voted for sold to you like so much cereal or soap? This revealing collection of essays is by political experts and specialists in opinion research, about the people who put across the "new politics" to the American public. The activities and techniques of campaign managers, advertising agencies, pollsters, public relations firms are examined and the result is "one of relevance and no-nonsense practicality. . . . Should be read by the new generation of young voters for its across-the-board know-how and candor." (*Publisher's Weekly*)

"This informative book is written without resort to unnecessary jargon. It should be of value both to political scientists and to the general, educated public."—*Library Journal*
ISBN 87491-314-4 (cloth)
  87491-315-2 (paper)
LCN 76-148048
312 pages / **$7.95**—cloth

INSIDE AMERICA:
A Black African Diplomat Speaks Out
by Fred Kwesi Hayford

Mr. Hayford is a Black man. But he is an African Black man—and there is a great difference between an African Black and an American Black. This is his candid and undiluted story about his own "culture shock" when he came to America as the Information Officer at the Embassy of Ghana in Washington, D.C.

He is blunt about the people—Black and white—about marriage and dating, about the Catholic Church, our dehumanizing technology, about the South. Trained to be objective and a diplomat, Fred Hayford felt finally that he must speak out about his "growing up in America" and INSIDE AMERICA is the result. America's streets may be "paved with gold," but is the price worth the reward? Read INSIDE AMERICA and see what you think.

". . . eyeopening are his views on American race and racism. Hayford sees white America so obsessed by a fear of black people that, in his view, virtually no real progress has been made at all. . . . He sees despair deepening and a violent outcome inevitable if American race relations are not improved on the human level."—*Publishers' Weekly*

"Americans convinced of the brotherhood of Blacks in America and Africa would do well to read these random recollections of life in the U.S."—*Library Journal*
ISBN 87491-326-8
LCN 78-184716
256 pages / **$6.95**—cloth

THE UNITED STATES vs WILLIAM LAITE
by W. E. Laite, Jr.

Rape, murder, assault, terror, indifference—it's all here as it is in other accounts by convicts of life in prison, but with a difference. The difference is that the convict could be you.

William Laite is a genial, round-faced, middle-class Georgia legislator, a respected citizen of Macon, and owner of a successful contracting business. His world collapses when he is accused of a wage-hour law violation.

Publishers' Weekly says: "His story covers his indictment, his trial, his legal battles to clear his name; but it is his eloquent portrayal of his personal shock and even terror in the brutal, venal and degrading prison world that makes his book a moving document."
. . . The book is another reminder of how slowly we learn the sanctity of human dignity among all individuals, including the outcasts who live out of sight behind the walls and bars in every county of the United States."
—*Washington Post*

"Readers may sneer at his prison service, less than five months of a year-and-a-day sentence. Those who sneer might try a little first-hand experience—say a half day in a holding cell for traffic violators. It doesn't take any longer to get the idea."
—*Miami Herald*
ISBN 87491-324-1
LCN 75-184718
250 pages / **$6.95**—cloth

ACROPOLIS BOOKS ON CURRENT ISSUES

acropolis books ltd.

2400 17th Street, N.W. (Courtyard) • Washington, D.C. 20009